THE THINGS WE DON'T KNOW

The Things We Don't Know

How mankind found answers to some of
life's most pressing questions.

TARUN BETALA

Book 1 of *A Shared Human Future* series

1st edition, July 31st, 2017

You can connect with the author at:

🌐 Email: tarun@tarunbetala.com
📘 Facebook: www.facebook.com/thethingswedontknowbook
🐦 Twitter: www.twitter.com/trbetala
📷 Instagram: www.instagram.com/tarunbetala
▶️Youtube: www.youtube.com/tarunbetala
🌐 Website: www.tarunbetala.com

Independently published by the author.

ISBN:

 Paperback (Asia & Latin America): 978-93-5279-670-0

 Paperback (North America & Europe): 978-197404266-1

 e-Book, Smashwords: 978-1-37-041992-0

To Rikki,

for giving me the courage to pursue the writing of this book
and for her constant feedback in making this possible

To my parents, Ratna and Roop,

who gave me the education and inclination to pursue knowledge
And who taught me how to be open minded and honest

To my sister, Ritika,

who listened to me blabber with excitement about my work
and who helped me spread the word

-this page intentionally left blank-

Contents

A Very Approximate Timeline

of historical events covered in this book

~6000 BCE	Jiahu Symbols were carved (Ch. 2)
~3000 BCE	First epic written by humans (Ch. 2)
	Cuneiform Script (Ch. 2)
	Enheduanna (Ch. 2)
~1500 BCE	First references to the Vedas (Ch. 6)
~0300 BCE	Alexandria established (Ch. 4)
~0200 BCE	Qin Shi Huang Unites China (Ch. 3)
~0050 BCE	Probable destruction of the Library of Alexandria (Ch. 4)
~0300 CE	Constantine unites Rome (Ch. 5)
	Christianity is *"legalized"* (Ch. 5)
~0500 CE	Buddhism and Jainism established (Ch. 6)
~0700 CE	The first ancient teaching institution, Nalanda, is established (Ch. 6)
~0800 CE	House of Wisdom is founded (Ch. 7)
~1200 CE	Nalanda is destroyed (Ch. 6)
~2015 CE	The Islamic State (IS) destroys a library in Mosul (Ch. 7)

Foreword

"I start with an idea and then it becomes something else"—Pablo Picasso

I accidentally bumped into this quote midway into the writing of *The Things We Don't Know,* and I couldn't relate to it any more than I already did. What started off as an account of the different theories of how our universe might operate, turned into a fusion of history, philosophy, and religion. I didn't expect this to be the end result but I couldn't be any more proud of what this work has become: an ode to the power of ideas, an account of the destruction of our knowledge and ideas, an in-exhaustive history of collaboration between societies of women and men, and the continuous perseverance of humanity to find out more about the world in which it lives.

A learning of history really does open up one's eyes

and brings light to the goodness of life as we live it. It shows us that some of the challenges we face today are recurring and universal and that humans throughout the course of history have been through, and do overcome, some of those challenges. We also realize that suppression of thought, and oppression of our beliefs is a recurring theme in different societies and different time periods, but more importantly, we learn that, time and again, we can and do overcome it.

If there is one thing the research of this book has shown, it is that barbaric, tyrannical, and ideological societies eventually stagnate. Thinkers of the past shed light to fallacies of our arrogance, and historical events shed light on what mistakes we must avoid. The world in which we live today is incredibly exciting, full of possibilities and contains answers to questions we didn't even know we should ask. It is the collective creative imagination and the drive of those who came before us that brought us to where we are. This should make us proud of who we've become; it should humble us because we've known some dark moments; it should make us aware of the gravity of the responsibility that has been given to us to do *something* with it.

A study of philosophy and religion helps in thinking about individual values—what do I care about? What are my beliefs? Do I blindly put my faith in others or do I question things and find answers that make sense to me? Some of these questions and others are answered in reading the thinkers and philosophies of the past. It also helps create a standard below which we wouldn't want our thoughts and actions to fall.

Philosophy doesn't have to be boring and theoretical. It can be uplifting, it can help us see the best in people and most of all, it can (and does) have practical applications, especially in the area of people and critical thinking skills. Religion doesn't have to be literal, it can be a guide to living a good life, to being compassionate, to propagating goodness. Besides, everybody has a core set of philosophies and beliefs of the why, what, and how of life. We just don't call these combined individual beliefs "religion".

Religion has had a turbulent history. People on both sides of the table—atheists and believers—have very strong reasons to support the points of view that they do. Collectively, we don't know the answer to whether religion is the be-all and end-all, let alone the ability to answer which religion is the most perfect representation of *god*, if any. We can't do much else but make peace with not knowing. We must be, and let others be, free to choose the beliefs that help make the best life for others and for ourselves; that freedom is our individual and collective *right*. War, oppression or shaming, on the other hand, isn't. It is a terrible side of humanity we still have to deal with. It is up to each of us to leave that side in the past—where it belongs. I'm painfully aware of the wars and the poverty that still plagues about a quarter of the world's population. Our species does still commit atrocities to their own kind under the banner of beliefs. We still harbor superstitious beliefs passed on to us over millennia. Even these, as compared to our past, are fewer in number. That doesn't make these actions any more acceptable. We ought to serve one another or get out of the way. But in the writing of this book, I have seen, as you will, the way in which we have grown up as a species, how we've evolved to this point in our collective narrative.

Some of the details in this book are intentionally vague. There was scope to include a lot more detail, especially around the lives of historic figures we've been introduced to over the course of this book. What we know of history is what is written down and passed on to us. In many cases, what was written and what really happened may not align. It is also possible that more than one factor contributed to some events; it is impossible to write a short book and an exhaustive history at the same time.

I've made some creative choices to eliminate or limit information that might otherwise make a story or idea lengthy and drawn out. It is a sincere hope that the reader takes the concept presented, rather than the literal interpretations of some of the events.

The incredibly vast internet and the willingness of people to share knowledge is mind blowing has been instrumental in understanding our past, speculating about our future and knowing what's going on around us. Since the following chapters are not complete histories, to find out more, one only needs to have the willingness to ask the right questions. In some cases, to give an idea of who's story we're in, you may either see a timeline of events or images of the people and concepts mentioned.

Considering the speed at which we operate and the number of things on our to do list, reflecting on the wonders of the present seems like a pipe dream. Reflect or not, wonderful it is, and this book is in part that reflection. A look at those wonders that we so often take for granted.

I consider this book, generally speaking, an introduction to some history, science, and philosophy rather than an in-depth analysis of the concepts involved. In order to keep the book interesting *enough,* some information is not included in the main text. More information can be found in either the footnotes or the appendix. Wikipedia, Reddit, Quora, as always, has been an invaluable guide and more detail can be found online. This is dangerous sometimes, as the information online is freely available and editable. It is our responsibility to validate facts and to ensure that the information we share on such a powerful platform is factual.

Towards the end of this book, there is a list of further recommended reading as a follow up, if this knowledge ignites further curiosity.

It is generally accepted that "she" is used when referring to a person positively, and "he" when referring to something that might be considered outside accepted social norms. Very superficially, in many cases, the pronouns used in this book are male—it isn't from the standpoint of segregating female readers, but out of convenience. Women play an amazing part in making our lives beautiful—they are simultaneously mothers, wives, sisters, creative thinkers, multitaskers, lovers and so much more. The history of "man", is really a history of humanity as a whole and not just the male species, and since some of it is so barbaric, *man* will do for now.

Lastly, there are artists, writers, and thinkers who have inspired me to write such a book as this. Carl Sagan, Richard Feynman, Sean Carroll, and Rumi, are just some of the names of people who are better writers, greater thinkers and more knowledgeable beings than I. I don't profess to know all about science or our history as a species. As they inspired me to learn more, to do more and to appreciate what the human mind is capable of, this is my effort at being a part of that universal conversation.

Their positivity inspired my work, their ideas inspired my words, and their hopes inspired my optimism. If those who read this book take away the interesting, unique and sometimes turbulent history of mankind, and of ideas, over the past six millennia, and feel interested in the concepts and ideas enclosed, I would consider myself successful. ∞

Chapter 1

How It All Came To Be

"Random chance plays a huge part in everybody's life."—Gary Gygax

On a fairly average evening, sitting in a café, a few of us were generally chatting about our day and sipping on some well-earned wine. One of us spoke about a conversation she had with her friends about how different things were a few years ago—her in college and how free she was while now it's about a few more responsibilities. Other conversations revolved around politics and the latest controversies, and some others related to our professional lives.

As is customary after a few glasses of wine, the conversation was led into the domain of the philosophical: this time around, it was about the cosmos and our place in it. We spoke about the different theories of how our universe came to be, and I mentioned how it saddens and thrills me at the same time. It is sad because we may never get to know the universe in which we live in totality, and it is thrilling to me because, though we do not know where we live on the grandest scale, we have so many theories. All of these theories seem to be simultaneously possible until one is proven right.

Some of our theories are, of course, more *probable* than others, but thinking about the different possibilities of the nature of our universe and our history is an immensely human act. We discover, invent, reflect, and think about our past and our future because we have the ability to do it—we have evolved to a point where our intelligence is not only helping us *ask these questions, but also answer some of them.* What a wonder it is—to speculate about what kind of a universe we inhabit, to learn and relearn what our history has been, to make plans about where we are going as a species and making it happen, to let our minds run free in the realm of unlimited and unchained possibilities.

How different each of our thought processes are: Similar people, at a similar point in life, thinking about things on completely different scales. The scales here do not represent any benefit—one interest is, generally speaking, no better than the other. We all just tend to be stimulated by different things. This difference, nonetheless, is something to cherish and enjoy. Both scales of the world are equal—what happens *there* happens *here*.

Letting alone the universe, it is impossible to even read all of our collective history as a species and understand it. There is so much literature, and so much of it is debatable, that following a true account of our evolution as members of a civilized world is an impossible task. We spoke about how even though it is impossible to know everything, the knowledge that we once had but don't have any more, is even more terrible: we have many references to historical events, people, and things, but we have accidentally or purposefully destroyed so much knowledge, that no reading of history can be truly complete. We spoke about how, sometimes serendipitously, we regain this knowledge quite by chance—through an excavation looking for something else, or a smuggler giving us ancient clay tablets. It was that chain of conversation on that very ordinary Friday evening in a cafe which led me to write this book.

*

On a human scale, we may be able to generalize. Some people like thinking about the world, some about politics, and some about the universe, while yet others enjoy watching and talking about sports. Marketing 101 emphasizes on knowing your customer. What they really mean is, knowing the segment of your customer. Males 18-25 like certain things. Females 50-60 like different things. If we are to advertise to one group of people—we ought to do it on certain platforms and not on others; we ought to do it a certain way and avoid others.

But on an individual level, no such generalization is

possible. If we are to truly appreciate the uniqueness of our thought and our individuality, the differences in our opinions must be celebrated. Over the course of human history, we bear witness to so many cases where good, great ideas were disregarded, suppressed or bullied because of their improbability because we had no means of proving them.

Some of our discoveries and inventions are accidents, some others are made in a moment of inspiration. Almost all of them are done individually or in teams, building upon the knowledge of our predecessors. But none of them would be possible if the environment wasn't right and the knowledge wasn't enough for those inventions.

Human beings, all of us, are amazing and temporal creatures in the grand scale of things. Billions of years in the making, we are one of the perfect specimens of evolution so far that the universe has been able to create so it can know itself. At least that we know of. Those who come after us may be a more perfect version of us—as we are a more perfect version of our ancestors far removed.

This is no reason to be arrogant, though—as we see through the ages, we are a part of the incredible process that perfects itself in no hurry whatsoever. With each iteration, our species—and the 8.7 million or so known species in the natural world—is able to better adapt to the world as we know it. And we, in turn, create new tools and think of new ideas that perfect those of our predecessors. From building fire from stones, we learned to make matches; from the abacus, the calculators; and from individual alphabets, the epics of literature.

It is our individuality—our opinions of the world, our opinions of dissent, of disagreements with the accepted and established order that got us here. Copernicus, Bruno, Einstein and so many others disagreed with what was the established view of the universe; some of them spent their entire lives trying to get others to see the world as they do. In these disagreements, we saw our first understandings of "truth"—of what can be observed and proved, rather than conjectured through religion, belief or what *we would like the world to be*.

It is in these differences of opinions that we understand what this world could be. It is in the observing and proving of some of these theories that we understand *what the world is*. ∞

Chapter 2

Look How Far We've Come

"Here's a question we all ask ourselves at least once when we're young: Where does that starlight come from? It's been there before I was born, and before my grandmother, and her grandmother were born. So just how far is that star from Earth?"—Kim Young-Ha

If we are to ask and answer questions about ourselves and the cosmos we inhabit, we must have the courage to 1) accept answers that we do not inherently agree with and 2) change our beliefs when evidence is provided to us that goes against our beliefs.

The way we perceive and consume the information in this world can be subjective, but there are some objective truths to our existence. Some of those objective truths in our universe or cosmos may be that the sun rises in the east, or that 2+2 equals four. These objective truths can be proved by observing the natural world. Upon observing an object, you may see that it is a certain color, and someone else looking at it may agree with your point of view. Some others may still say that it's not white but cream, or not brown but chestnut, and they may be right.

In that sense, we all collectively agree on certain things. That the color "blue" is indeed what we call "blue" and that if you have two potatoes, you have exactly one potato and then one more. These are names we give our concepts. The concept of having one and one more of something is "two" and so on.

So when we talk about 2+2 = 4, what we really are saying is that the nature of two added to the nature of another two gives us the nature of four, and this is true regardless of what thing we are talking about. *Two of anything twice is four of that thing*.

The understanding of the difference between concepts and what we name them is important: What we call four in English is *chaar* in Hindi, *cuatro* in Spanish and *quatre* in French. The nature of "four" doesn't change even if we call it by different names.

*

We don't *really* have a sense of our history. What we know is fragmented and deduced based on the information available in some records—whether it is looking at the oldest piece of rock and deducing that the earth is 4.5 billion years old, or looking at the fossils and deducing that dinosaurs once roamed the earth, or reading the writings and symbols left to us by those who came before us. We can speak of an approximate timeline from the beginning of the universe until today, but fragments of time are lost to us, and in some cases, we have conflicting accounts of what really happened. These conflicting accounts sometimes give us insight into the different ways events may have been perceived. In other cases, history may have been rewritten by those who had the ability and the willingness to rewrite it.

What we have deduced, deciphered and recovered so far, however, is nothing short of amazing. We have, as a species, come up with a way to look at a piece of rock and tell exactly how old that rock is. We call this process radiocarbon dating. We have deciphered ancient scripts—Egyptian Hieroglyphics, for instance—and understood how life might have been for the Egyptians. We have pieced together a development of our history using disparate sources, conjecturing what mattered to our ancestors.

We know how and what they thought about gods, life, the stars, food and animals. We approximately know how each culture lived and how they developed some of our most prized beliefs. We know at least a part of what they passed down to us. We have created techniques to deduce how old a rock is; we can look at a whole host of rocks and fossils and effectively trace a story or a timeline out of it. We can read the books left to us and know *how* we know what we know. We can immerse ourselves through our knowledge in the past, and create a picture of what happened. If anything is time traveling, this is it.

We know how our ancestors lived, how they thought, invented and discovered. The art of the past—inscriptions, paintings, and sculptures—show us how people may have looked, how they dressed, what they saw. Our collective imagination jumps in and fills in the other details that we can't conclusively prove yet, creating an image of each moment of our history as a species. The corpus of our knowledge helps us relive the past, even if only in our minds, and the more we discover, the more we learn about the past and understand it.

Why do we care so much about rocks and history, though? It is one way to deduce our past as inhabitants of this world. How did we come to be? How were things before *now*? It all started with studying and observing the universe—and our world—and its contents as they are. What we see around us today are remnants of the past. We are able to create certain things today because of the creations of the past. They are records of what existed before us, and these fragments of knowledge tell us where we came from: they tell us the story of our becoming.

This is possible because of thousands of years of theorizing, making scientific discoveries, creating objects that can make our lives easier—from the first light bulb to the spaceship in which we explore *our home*. The spaceship is not an individual feat—if electricity was not discovered by the ancients, advanced further by Benjamin Franklin in the mid-1700s[1], and the electric bulb not created by Thomas Edison in 1879, spaceships, our computers, industrialization and our modern life would not be possible. Perhaps someone else, later on in our timeline would discover it. Perhaps it wouldn't come to be for another hundred or thousand years until the next inventor came along.

Imagine this: it took about two hundred years from the discovery of the nature of electricity to creating the first light bulb. But to go from the light bulb to the spaceship only took us three hundred years! This is a testament to the power of our cumulative knowledge and the importance of the knowledge of the past. Learning from our predecessors compounds our knowledge. If we didn't learn from those who came into this world and discovered how the world worked, we would not be able to apply those findings to create a better future. We would be destined to reinventing the wheel and rediscovering fire with each new generation that came along. A reflection on our past shows us that our minds are evolution in action: as our DNA makes lovely, amazing mistakes and course corrects, so do our minds.

The spaceship, for instance, or any advance in our species—is a part of the sum of all the knowledge that we gathered as a species over a period of time. The spaceship may be created in the 21st century but the knowledge and the tools that enabled us to do it today were created years, centuries, in some cases millennia ago. We are able to accomplish today what our ancestors had hoped, dreamed and prayed for.

We ought to be incredibly grateful for this legacy. We live in an age where information is ever present. I googled concepts more than a hundred times while I was writing this book—what is the correct grammar for certain words? What is the process of studying the earth called? (Geology), what should I have for dinner? and so on. There are scientists, doctors, researchers, entrepreneurs and engineers working today, finding innovative applications for already existing inventions, creating new and marvelous objects to make our life easier, and theorizing for the future that will someday help create things we can only dream of. In that very limited sense, our legacy lives on for longer than we do. In some cases, for millennia.

An unbelievable imagination is the greatest gift this universe has given us, and access to knowledge, through documenting events and ideas, is one of the greatest gifts our species has given itself. Before the interconnectedness of the world, before the internet, data, information, knowledge were not always omnipresent, and yet, people from the ages built on years of theory and practice to come up with the world that we have today. This understanding was definitely not lost on our predecessors.

So it is curious and truly saddening to think about the books that were banned, or worse, burned throughout our history. We understood the value and rarity of knowledge, and we simultaneously managed to find ways to oppress it. We are products of the environment in which we grow up. If it isn't for society, we might have to still make our own food—from scratch. Imagine *refining* sugar, milking a cow, roasting a coffee bean for a hot cup of latte—and that's just the drink. We have three more whole meals to go. Society helps us be *relatively* independent, be *relatively* free, preserve and propagate culture and knowledge, and move our species forward. Individuals innovate—people see how things could be better and they affect change, and these individuals are able to do it because of society; because of continuity of our society and our species. How, then, do individuals in this same interconnected ecosystem manage to oppress, bully, kill and destroy?

Another loss, one which we have no control over, is the loss of our knowledge to time. We may never learn about the ideas, artifacts, writings, and people that we have lost to time because we don't have any way of knowing what they are. But for better or for worse, there is immense knowledge that we *do have,* and we may take heart in the fact that in a human lifetime, we may never be able to read all that we want to read, understand all the concepts we want to understand, and experience all that we want to experience. The brevity of human life basically ensures that we may never be able to know all that there is to know, no matter how vicariously we live.

And yet, in about six thousand years, we've gone from a few words depicting daily events to a plethora of knowledge, the accumulation of which only immortality may be the cure. In early 2003, archeologists discovered writings on tortoise shells in the Jiahu province of China. These shells date back to around the seventh millennium BCE, where one researcher suggests that they were used for cultural rituals. These symbols are one of the earliest records of writings we have found so far. The culture during that period does not appear to require a writing system, so what we see is symbols representing everyday objects—the eye, a window, and a couple of numerals. It is entirely possible that writing before this period has not yet been discovered or that some of the early civilizations wrote on temporary surfaces and those may be writings lost to time.

Another early record of writing emerged in both Mesopotamia (modern day Iraq and Kuwait) and Egypt[2] around 3500 BCE. What a brilliant way to remember things— to write them down! The significance of this writing is not limited. One such early record of writings, called the *cuneiform script,* gives us a sense of the life and thoughts of our predecessors. In reading the history of cuneiform and the subsequent decryption of the script, we see not only the development of the language but also the increased need for communicating ideas through writing with *exactness.*

The earlier cuneiform writings were pictorial, depicting everyday things— sheep, gods, kings, floods and material things. This kind of writing was simple and portrayed only simple ideas, but from these material depictions of visible objects, the Mesopotamians, who developed and widely used what we call the cuneiform, moved on to depict ideas and concepts that couldn't necessarily be explained through pictures. To show someone what a table means, one may point to a table—but to explain to them hunger or love or loneliness, more complex form of writing needs to be developed.

> "All that had been devised thus far was a technique for noting down things, items and objects, not a writing system. A record of `Two Sheep Temple God Inanna' tells us nothing about whether the sheep are being delivered to, or received from, the temple, whether they are carcasses, beasts on the hoof, or anything else about them"—Paul Kriwaczek

Over the course of a few millennia, cuneiform developed from a script depicting simple material objects to an ancient literary tradition with mythologies and epics that are still awe-inducing today. One such work, *The Epic of Gilgamesh* is one of the oldest and grandest of literary works, addressing such universal human themes as immortality, friendship, life and death, love and lust among others. Even so, the epic spans only twelve tablets with modern retellings lasting for about 70 or so pages.

Though what we have recovered from it is still incomplete, we do know a fair bit of the contents, the mythological world, and the storyline. Even this knowledge of the storyline of the epic is marvelous! We not only deciphered what was written in a completely different script with few superficial characteristics in common with our current written languages, but we also pieced together a work from nearly four thousand years ago from different sources.

Cuneiform writings [3]

Five Sumerian poems formed different parts of the story and were written much before the epic. These are considered to be the source material for the eventual combined single work. In modern translations, any information not in either of these two sources are either left blank or story points are created by the translator so as to create a smooth, flowing narrative for a better reading experience. Our knowledge of this ancient culture and the epic is dynamic; we still find new story points which give the ancient mythical world more color and depth.

Serendipitously, our newest knowledge was found in the unlikeliest of places: the most recent discovery was made when, in 2015, a smuggler tried to sell 80 or so clay tablets to a museum in Kurdistan in Iraq. It is poetic how a war-torn nation manages to give us mythical knowledge that was lost for most of recorded history.

The presence of mind of a professor of languages at the museum, Al-Rawi, ensured that we know more about our beloved Babylonian mythological world than we ever did. As far as the story goes, we have additional detail regarding the cedar forest of the gods. Previously supposed to be quiet and peaceful, the forest is actually noisy and often disturbed by monkeys; It is, of course, impossible to convey the depth and the influence of this work in a few pages (which is strived for any way at the end of this book in the appendix), but as far as fiction is concerned, the world is in the details, and a few lines can dramatically change the way we perceive an important element of this ancient mythological world. And if that world is the first fictional world ever created, every detail matters:

"What Al-Rawi and George translated is a formerly unknown portion of the fifth tablet, which tells the story of Gilgamesh, king of Uruk, and Enkidu (the wild man created by the gods to keep

Gilgamesh in line) as they travel to the Cedar Forest (home of the gods) to defeat the ogre Humbaba.

The new tablet adds 20 previously unknown lines to the epic story, filling in some of the details about how the forest looked and sounded.

The new tablet continues where other sources break off, and we learn that the Cedar Forest is no place of serene and quiet glades. It is full of noisy birds and cicadas, and monkeys scream and yell in the trees." 4

Perhaps more importantly, and more pertinent to our world today, we find that even the Babylonians cared for their forests and that even in our early years, cutting down forests to create wastelands was considered to "upset the gods":

"Gilgamesh and Enkidu cut down the cedar to take home to Babylonia, and the new text carries a line that seems to express Enkidu's recognition that reducing the forest to a wasteland is a bad thing to have done, and will upset the gods"

In a span of thousand years, early civilizations not only created conceptual writing but also created an imaginative work of literature that rivals and influences many stories even today. These discoveries bring to light one more fundamental fact about humanity: that the human emotions of happiness, of loss, of grief, of fear of death are both recurring and universal themes in our species, and that time and again, we are forced to relive our own personal histories and face these fears.

These antediluvian writings also show us something else: a look at the development of cuneiform is also a look at the development of our own knowledge as a species. The same way in which the cuneiform paved the way to the development of five poems, which were then developed to make the epic, our disparate knowledge in different fields comes together to form a synergy, producing a result greater than the sum of its parts. The famous story of Noah's Ark, for instance, is remarkably close, in almost all story points, to the ancient flood story discussed in the Epic of Gilgamesh.

In reading the flood stories, one cannot help but remark at the similarities presented: a man is warned of a great flood that will destroy the whole world. He then builds a vast boat and saves two of each species, and after a long flood, he releases a bird to find dry land. It is possible that religious and cultural literature was built upon stories that were passed orally. In the same way that the development of writing help the creation of the *epic,* the creation of the epic affected the future developments of stories told to mankind.

But stories being adapted by different cultures is one thing. Disparate sources coming together to form something new is another. Astrophysics, for instance, combines our knowledge of two apparently unrelated sciences—physics and chemistry—and helps us explain the birth and death of planets, galaxies and other objects in the universe. It is because we are able to overlay two or more different subjects, that we exponentially increase our understanding of our universe. Without both Chemistry and Physics, and our ability to connect the dots, much of our distant universe would be unknown and alien to us.

But *The Epic of Gilgamesh* is not the only thing the Sumerians gave us, though one could hardly ask for more from so foundational a culture. It is during this period that we also find the first written record of a religion in the world. If human beings asked questions about our place in the universe before this period, and deduced that gods must have created us, we have no records of it.

This is also the time and place that gave us our very first author. Shakespeare, Dickens, Twain, and Rowling are all preceded by one woman—Enheduanna, the first author that we have a record of so far. The life of Enheduanna itself is fascinating: She is the first woman to have the role of the "high-priestess of the temple of Ur", which is what Enheduanna translates to. She was once exiled by a king who tried to create a coup but she returned to the temple as the high-priestess. While in exile, she wrote the following hymn to the god An to petition her return:

"Funeral offerings were brought, as if I had never lived there.

I approached the light, but the light scorched me.
I approached the shade, but I was covered with a
storm.
My honeyed mouth became scummed. Tell An about
Lugal-Ane and my fate!
May An undo it for me! As soon as you tell An about
it, An will release me."

Poems such as these seem to have been her forte. Enheduanna is not just the first author but also one of the earliest women that we know of. She wrote devotional poems for Innana, a Sumerian goddess of sex, beauty, fertility among other things; she also composed temple hymns that have influenced prayers to the present day. The hymns that she wrote to the goddess Inanna, and the moon god Nanna gave the Sumerian people a deeper understanding of the character of these gods.

While the general populace considered gods to be threatening or intimidating, Enheduanna's works brought a layer of compassion to these gods and reconciled the differences in Sumerian and Accadian gods. This intellectual innovation brought people closer to understanding their relation with the gods of the time and helped create more stability in the Sumerian empire.

Peering into this time period gives us a clue into the focus of literary works in the Sumerian world. Most ancient writings from the culture revolve around the relationship of man and god but the significance of a culture can hardly be explained by a few works emerging in that culture, though the Epic of Gilgamesh and Enheduanna's poems do stand out for their respective imaginative narrative. The Sumerian and other Mesopotamian cultures, just like diverse cultures today, wondered about our place in the world, interacted with each other—sometimes not constructively—and prayed, hoped and looked for answers.

*

Deciphering languages is no easy feat. With no prior knowledge of the Japanese language and the script, imagine being given a set of Japanese texts and being asked to decipher it. How many of us would be able to collectively do it, and how long that process would take! Modern scripts that make up words, which make up sentences and so on, were invented sometime around 800 BCE and gained prominence only around 100 BCE. In the two-hundred-year history of the decipherment of cuneiform[5], we still course correct as new information is found, and for all that we *do know* about cuneiform, there are scripts that remain indecipherable even today.

From the earliest Jiahu symbols of the seventh millennium BCE, to at least the 13th century CE, we have records of more than 30 undecipherable scripts. One such script called the Wadi el-Hol script remains undecipherable. Found in Egypt by Yale archeologists, it is suggested that this script may be an early transition from hieroglyphic to an alphabetic system. The contents of the inscriptions, however, elude us.

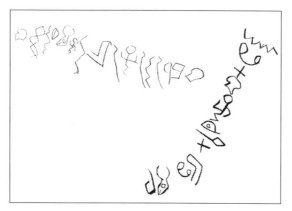

Wadi el-Hol script [6]

We can perhaps take heart in the fact that all of our thoughts, all of our philosophies recur in many different forms and in many different cultures. The variety and sheer number of human viewpoints and opinions should almost guarantee that we have thought everything there is to think about—but how can one ever be sure?

What humans discover over a period of time or at the same time in different places also duplicate. Writing in Egypt and Mesopotamia developed around the same time; the idea of a soul is practically omnipresent; gods having created and caring for us is a basis of many cultures. When our environment and evolution brings us to a certain point, our thoughts are derivations of either what we think or how we feel, so it's not surprising that civilizations halfway across the world may develop similar social, religious, and economic structures.

Mark Twain famously quipped that all ideas are second hand, "consciously and unconsciously drawn from a million outside sources, and daily used by the garnerer with a pride and satisfaction born of the superstition that he originated them"[7]. That which is lost for once might be found again at a different time by a different individual. That's the great thing about humanity: we are one in our search. Our search for freedom, for answers, for truth, for meaning. ∞

Chapter 3

The Early Lost Knowledge

"Humans have both the urge to create and destroy."—Hayao Miyazaki

While in time, we may recreate ideas lost, there is a more depressing side to this story. Throughout human history, we've fiercely opposed and oppressed any idea that challenges our worldview. It takes courage to accept something that we inherently don't agree with. We explore worlds, we write for our progeny, we create engineered and artistic wonders, and yet, conversations based on facts take ridiculously long to become accepted norm. In the process, we take destructive action to oppress or suppress new ideas for the sake of the stability of our societies and the security of our own belief systems.

It is not improbable that since we've been able to

think and communicate, there have been a subset of people who have felt threatened. Since we started writing, there have been those of us who wished to destroy the writing. We hardly have a complete record of what we wrote, let alone what we destroyed.

Records of our history of book burnings start in the 2nd century BCE in China[8], when Qin Shi Huang conquered the six other warring states in the general region we now know as China and unified it under his empire. The Qin dynasty, phonetically pronounced 'chin', showed us the first inklings of what China would later become: An imperial state with a highly structured political power, a stable economy, and a large military which used the most advanced weaponry and military techniques of the time.

For four centuries leading up to the Qin dynasty, free thought was implicitly encouraged and many diverse religions, philosophies, and schools of thought formed[9], each suggesting and detailing how man ought to live, behave and interact in the world. The period from 6th century BCE to mid-2nd century BCE saw the inception and growth of incredibly diverse—and in many cases, opposing— philosophies. Later called the "hundred schools of thought" era, this time period gave rise to such popular oriental philosophies as Confucianism and Taoism, and these philosophies have seen a new wave of discovery and adoption in recent times.

Not only did philosophers openly criticize each other

during this period, but they also had a direct influence on the coexistence of these philosophies. Each of the seven warring states patronized philosophers, scholars, and teachers, who competed with each other for the attention of their rulers and devised different social, economic and political philosophies.

In order to spread their beliefs, there was an increased emphasis, for the first time, on the recording of the teachings and philosophies into books. This competition between the scholars may also have led to developing philosophies that were inherently practical. Any philosophy which was conjectural and didn't have immediate practical application didn't gain prominence.

The conversations in these religious philosophies were related to ethics, politics, social structures, strategies to win at war and increasing power, among other things. These topics were within the realm of what man could concern himself with immediately, and so each of these philosophies were chiefly concerned with the doings of man.

Each school of thought during the time developed its own system of how man should operate within the confines of a society and what is or isn't right for him to do. Some philosophies focused on morals, some on the common man, others on politics, and yet others didn't bother with any morality or the common man at all. Instead, they focused solely on achieving economic growth and stability.

This diversity of opinion was responsible for immense intellectual and cultural growth in the region, each learning from, and critiquing, another.

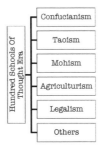

*The different philosophies that emerged during the
intellectual expansion in China, pre-Qin dynasty*

Confucianism, for instance, encouraged meritocracy,
though it wasn't the only one: the status of an individual must
be determined by his education and character, and not by his
wealth or relationships. In a world where blood relations
granted an advantage, this was a revolutionary idea. It was
less a religion than a way of life, focusing on the virtues a man
must develop in order to live his best life under the banner of
heaven. The core of Confucianism lies in the belief that human
beings are fundamentally good and able to improve
themselves to attain virtuousness, and by extension,
"oneness" with "heaven".

Confucianism suggests that this self-improvement
should be the end-goal of all men in all affairs of life—whether
in political or familial life. Men must develop themselves by
the following of virtues such as benevolence, righteousness,
integrity, loyalty and so on.

This philosophy is very humanist in its approach, like many other Chinese philosophies of the time. In early forms of Confucianism literature and practice, there were no spiritual explanations to life after death, karmic, heavenly or hellish influences on our life. There were gods, but these were in the form of no Abrahamic god who looks after, judges, creates, shuns, and cares. These gods were impersonal but "gave us life". A supernatural force, *"Tian"*, can be roughly translated as the nature of "the universe" or "the way things are in our world".

This makes the grouping of Confucianism with other Abrahamic religions confusing since there are no equivalent spiritual explanations as to the creation of the world and a supernatural meaning of our existence. In fact, early Confucian texts weren't interested in ultimate questions and focus instead on what man can do and know. Rituals, for example, are strongly encouraged in Confucianism because they bring the family and community together towards the same goal.

Confucius, inspired by the history of China, sought to revive the moral values that made an earlier Chinese empire, the Zhou dynasty, so successful. He saw himself less as a prophet than as a transmitter of the values of what he saw as the "golden period" of Chinese culture. He concerned himself with the importance of the virtuousness of man in every aspect of his life: Only by governing virtuously can a king be fit to rule over his empire; only by living honestly can men live a happy and a prosperous life.

A co-existing philosophy, Taoism found its roots in the hundred schools of thought era as well. Like Confucianism, Taoism cannot be studied like the Abrahamic religions—the followers of the Tao may also believe in concepts shared by other contemporary religious philosophies. A Confucian may actually also be a Taoist, so to speak.

"Tao", like *"Tian"*, can also be interpreted as "the way things are" or the "natural order of the universe". The core concept propagated by the Taoist philosophy is that individuals should seek to find a harmony with the universe and their actions should be "effortless" rather than "forced". What was originally seen as the religion of the hermits and wandering philosophers was eventually canonized and called "Taoism", but in a general sense, there is no such thing as a Taoist. A follower of Taoism could be anyone following the general principles propagated by Taoism.

It is not the belief that makes a Taoist, but rather his actions and their alignment with nature. These actions are five-fold: spontaneity, simplicity, detachment from desires, effortless action, and naturalness.

Although both Confucian and Taoist texts talk about oneness and focus on rituals that are important to the society, there are some key differences in their philosophies. Unlike Confucianism, Taoism doesn't believe that a social order is necessary for a successful society. While Confucianism believes in the division of labor and a respect for positions of authority, Taoism propagates a sense of equality and oneness with nature, and that any man-made social structures are only temporary, and therefore, not necessary to be in harmony with nature. Confucianism focuses heavily on politics, how kings must rule virtuously and how a strong sense of community can create a better life for all; in Taoism, there is no focus on politics and virtually no importance given to a political life.

Mohism, also a contemporary philosophy to Taoism and Confucianism, takes this "oneness" to a whole new level. Mohist philosophers go so far as to suggest that man must practice "universal love", and that we must love strangers as we love our blood relatives. This kind of oneness has been re-invented over and over at different times and in different cultures by different people.

Such musicians as Bob Marley and John Lennon sang of our shared oneness. Rumi, the Islamic 8th-century Sufi poet, wrote of oneness of the world. Eckhart Tolle & Dalai Lama write about our oneness with the soul of the world. These recurring themes of universal love in different cultures and different times in our society say something about our shared need for peace. Mohism is one early representation of our desires for world peace and universal love. It didn't value warfare and advocated frugality to the extreme. It was—if anything—a philosophy which advocated the ascetic lifestyle for the common people.

In thinking about the impracticality of loving everyone alike, reject warfare and living ridiculously frugally, it is easy to see why Mohism as a philosophy had a limited appeal. It found ample criticism from its contemporaries, in that climate of open dialogue, and it faded out quite naturally, unlike Taoist and Confucian philosophies.

One example of extreme frugality is the Mohist stance on music. In Mohism, music is considered to be wasteful and opulent, and therefore, not necessary. In thinking about examples such as these, it is easy to see why the popularity of Mohism effectively declined. Not having music as an art form would indeed be a loss for humanity. Some of the greatest pleasures in life cannot be explained and must be felt. Music, in some cases, is an expression of the things we can sense and feel, but find hard to explain.

As most schools criticized and learned from one another, so the concept of the *Tao* and the importance of rituals were adopted by most philosophical schools of the period. Chinese religious philosophies of the time actually looked to find unity in the practice of different philosophies over time. It is fairly easy to reconcile Abrahamic and Chinese religions—technically, one can be a Christian or a Muslim and Confucian at the same time.

But for all the practicality, religion was mired with pseudoscience, a belief in superstition and the supernatural. Believers often practiced ritualistic sacrifices and had certain places and times where sacrifices and rituals must be performed in order to be most effective. Alchemical formulas that outlined how one ought to achieve immortality were also outlined in Taoism, so an outline of only the practicality of these philosophies is not a complete representation.

In the reading of these religions and current renewed interest in ancient religions, one outstanding difference is that we are now relatively more accepting of the fact that certain things are unknowable, and don't find it necessary to create superstitious beliefs in order to answer the unanswerable. Superstitions and spiritual conversations today are fairly different from the times of our ancestors, but without their beliefs, and the subsequent questioning of those beliefs, we wouldn't be in a position to know as much as we do.

In the midst of this cultural and intellectual growth, Qin united China and enforced legalism as *the* "religion" of the state: Laws must be followed, and any transgressions will be penalized. To think of the law as a religion might seem strange, but it's not a very different view when compared to conventional religions. Religions across the board have "laws" that must be followed or else face the wrath of the gods; some early religions made no causal relationships between man's actions and god's wrath.

Qin undoubtedly had a vision for his grand unified kingdom. Self-proclaimed *The Emperor of China*, he aimed to create an empire that would be greater than any before its time, and Qin would be its ruler. It was this vision that led to the destruction of what Qin would otherwise have for its progeny.

This new unified empire was aimed at standardizing not only the currency, units of measurements, and the writing systems, but also the empire's way of life, and subsequently the thought process of its citizens. Up until Qin's conquest of the region, China was divided into factions, with different kingdoms overseeing different regions, laying down somewhat different laws, and operating with different currencies, distinct measurement standards, and varied writing systems. As with any new system, there was opposition and criticism to the new way of life. With the empire's will and the ability to wield power over the population, he sought to effectively unify thought and political opinion.

This unity of thought and public opinion would ensure that the people of China would view the current system favorably. Qin exerted power to preserve power and protect dissent. The initial goodness of intention to "teach and lead people, rid them of dissoluteness and depravity... and turn them toward goodness"[10] turned into an authoritarian regime in a no-win situation.

Any subversive thoughts, philosophies, and history of life before the Qin dynasty were considered to be threats to the current system and were supposedly destroyed[11]. Qin expected to preserve two copies of each book of the different philosophies in the imperial libraries which were also destroyed towards the end of the Qin dynasty. Scholars were urged to submit all books that didn't align with the enforced philosophy of the empire—"legalism"—to be burnt.

Anyone who didn't submit, or kept such information about literature from the authorities were sentenced to death. This event, later called the "Burning of books and burying of scholars", essentially put an end to the interactions and the open debates between the different philosophical schools in China. The two decades following the unification of China saw some intellectual growth, but very little cultural stimulation. For the rulers, though, legalism worked. It gave greater control to the aristocracy and ensured relative stability within their kingdom.

The philosophical basis of legalism was grounded in skepticism about the intentions of men and gave them very little benefit of doubt. It focused little on virtues or morals, took the view that men are inherently self-interested and that the law's role is to induce order and justice by punishing or rewarding the actions of men. Only by ensuring stability in the society can a ruler restore order to the world.

As far as Legalism was concerned, a ruler ought to ensure stability by building a stronger government, increasing the production of food, enforce military training and strategically increase his power bases. The legitimacy or fairness of these courses mattered very little. The stability and growth of the society was of prime importance, and the way to a stable society was by the strict enforcement of the laws.

So, when Qin destroyed all philosophies that weren't

aligned with legalism, he may have destroyed any chance of us receiving cultural and intellectual input from one of the earliest civilizations created by man. If it wasn't for the (sometimes disputed) *records of the grand historian (called Shiji)*, all knowledge from this time period would be lost.

Qin Shi Huang, the First Emperor of a Unified China[12]

We would have no idea about the philosophies of a group which called themselves the agriculturists: those who believed that the ruler must tend to his farm alongside everyone else in the society. An agriculturist king is not outside of realm of the farms and doesn't lead from the top, and neither does he inflict hardship upon his subjects in order to increase his wealth. Agriculturism in China is probably the first classless and egalitarian society that we know of—where all the citizens of that society were considered to be equal, and there was no division of labor based on the status of the individual.

None of the literature on Agriculturism survives, and all that we know of it comes from the criticism it received from its contemporaries, which were recorded in the *Shiji*.

We are also introduced to the "school of minor-talks", which was effectively the philosophy of the common people. A thought had by the common people, of the common people combined to make this whole philosophy, for the common people. Perhaps we see the seeds of "social media" of the time here. But why must we care so much about the different philosophies? There are two major reasons why these schools of thoughts need to be understood in the context of Chinese, and human, history.

First, as we see later in the 2nd century BCE, only one religion—legalism—was "allowed". For almost four centuries before this time, multitudes of religions coexisted. Scholars, teachers, and philosophers were patronized and competed to come up with philosophies that would stabilize and advance the state and perhaps help conquer the other six states. The goal of progress was to stabilize the region, control more land, and unite more regions under the banner of one kingdom.

Before the Qin dynasty's enforcement of legalism, an individual who practiced Confucianism might also practice Taoism, depending on the role he was exhibiting. As a soldier, he may abide by the Confucian philosophy of hierarchy and may honor established roles. Outside of *work*, he may exhibit the Taoist need for being one with the nature of the world. To reconcile two philosophies depending on the role one is exhibiting is an incredibly progressive trait and not something we easily associate with early history of man.

Second, the people had freedom of practice and of thought. They were, relatively speaking, free to practice any or none of the different philosophies of the time until Qin took over and sought to organize and homogenize action and thought. When Qin decided to homogenize thoughts, he did so for the sake of the stability for their empire. If there would be no deviation of thought, all of Qin's kingdom would work towards the same goals: conquering more land, producing more food and so on. This single-mindedness would mean fewer transgressions and less time spent on managing the internal affairs of the empire while looking outward and spreading the rule.

In this creation of a new way of life, he burnt almost all of the literature on the hundred schools of thought. The two copies expected to be preserved in a single location were burnt in a fire, effectively destroying much of recorded thought that developed over the five centuries of Chinese history. But in a practical sense, Confucianism had generally been infused into the Chinese way of life, such that even after the binding legalism of the state, Confucian values of filial piety[13] and ritualistic sacrifice, among other things continued to be assumed by the citizens.

Of course, not all of Qin's actions were oppressive or

harmful to the society. In uniting China, Qin also created a model of rule that would be followed by succeeding kingdoms for generations. Qin created standardized measurement systems, currency, homogenized the Chinese script, and created an extensive road network to improve trade between the different provinces. He also unified what we know now as the Great Wall of China. The warring states had already walled their kingdoms; Qin's main contribution to this was the unifications of these state walls. Though much the original "unified" wall doesn't remain, what we see today was rebuilt later around the 13th century. The question that begs to be asked here is whether the kind of oppression and loss of knowledge was necessary to accomplish what Qin and his rule did.

After the fall of the Qin dynasty, which lasted for a mere 15 years, the Han dynasty took center stage, ushering a four-century long period of economic prosperity. Different religions were allowed to exist, the law code and the model of the kingdom was essentially borrowed from Qin's rule. The records of the Grand Historian—sometimes questionable in its propaganda against Qin—comes from the Han dynasty. Most of what we know about the Chinese history, its philosophies and its way of life can be credited to this period.

Qin is said to have been severely afraid of his death and ironically died on his way to seek an elixir which would grant him immortality. We may never know what alternate route Chinese history, and consequently our world history, may have taken if it wasn't for the two-decade oppression that was brought on by Qin.

*

The Chinese society was far in advance of the rest of the world until the 14th century. Historian Mark Elvin describes why China never underwent an industrial revolution with a concept called high-level equilibrium trap. The theory postulates that the supply and demand of the region were in the balance, and that the trade networks and labor was so cheap that there was no motivation to invest capital to and improve efficiency: it would be unprofitable.

Further, Confucianism was adopted as the state religion, along with legalism. Taoism promoted an inquiry into the natural sciences and mathematics. As we see later, Christian monks (and largely the western scientists) saw inquiry into the natural sciences as a way of understanding god, and our world with it. Confucianism, on the other hand, was more concerned with moral and social philosophy. This created a system that wasn't conducive to technical innovations and focused instead on the social sciences[14]. ∞

Chapter 4

A Beacon of Our Knowledge

"Our good life in Alexandria was brief, but how potent were the perfumes, how splendid the bed on which we lay, and to what sensual delights did we give our bodies to?"—from Collected Poems by Constantinos P. Cavafis

One of the more magnificent stories about the history of our knowledge revolves around a library, as it probably should. Any history of our cultural, economic, and scientific growth and of our knowledge is incomplete without the mention and detailing of the library of Alexandria. It is a beacon of the pursuit of knowledge and the manifestation of our desire to understand, collect, organize and share what we know.

After the demise of Alexander the Great in 323 BCE, his successor, Ptolemy I took control of the city of Alexandria, and founded there a library, with a goal to have 500,000 scrolls within its walls. At its peak, the city of Alexandria was the intellectual and cultural center of the world, and the Alexandrian library is reported to have close to half a million papyrus scrolls by some accounts.

Alexandria was one of the largest cities of its time and the largest in Egypt. It is considered to be "the first city of the civilized world in size, elegance, riches, and luxuries". People from around the world came to Alexandria in search of material and spiritual prosperity. Trade was abundant and so was the ability to purchase anything one might desire at the time.

It was at this time that the average man didn't need to have a political opinion, didn't need to worry about fighting in wars. Mercenary armies were armies of soldiers who fought for private gain, for money, and were the norm in this new world[15]. With no need to think or worry about fighting wars, the common man of Alexandria focused on art, spirituality, philosophy, mathematics and even religion. [16]

And so, it became one of the leading cultural centers of the third century and perhaps the first city where men and women of different faiths all shared a common land in an effort to cultivate a better livelihood. Men from different backgrounds visited and migrated to Alexandria too: philosophers, mathematicians, scientists, poets all had a part to play in the cultural capital of Alexandria.

Our knowledge of the contents and an exhaustive

history of the library is, however, limited. The index of the books that were in the library is said to have disappeared with the destruction of the library, but it is in this library that the first catalog of books was created[17]. We live in a world where information is available almost instantly, so it may not seem like a catalog of books in a library is innovative, but for almost 2 millennia, catalogs of books didn't exist. From the first library in Sumer in the 3rd millennium BCE, until the 3rd century BCE—about 2300 years—we didn't have a way to categorize, organize and retrieve books systematically. It was, if you will, the Google of the time. Very loosely, what the catalog was to books, Google is to web pages.

It was just a matter of time for such an innovation to come to exist. Given enough scrolls, the need for a list of the scrolls in the library would be evident, and any innovative and resourceful librarian would create one. Perhaps we didn't feel the need for a catalog until such an ambitious project as the Alexandrian Library was undertaken. With the amount of time it takes to scour a library manually, this process of cataloging all the books made access to knowledge relatively effortless and was an incredible tool for intellectuals and scholars to navigate the seas of vast knowledge that was stored in Alexandria.

The library was a center of many other firsts too. Eratosthenes, a mathematician and later a head librarian at Alexandria, was the first person to have scientifically calculated the circumference of the earth. Almost 2300 years ago, with absolutely no modern scientific instruments but a keen knowledge of geometry and an innovative streak. He may also have been the inventor of the leap day—the 366th day we observe every four years.

Some of the greatest intellectual minds of the time came to Alexandria in search of meaning for their work. Aristarchus was the first person known to have suggested that the earth might revolve around the sun, almost two thousand years before we could prove and accept it! Incidentally, Copernicus' theory wasn't new when he put it forward; the possibility of a heliocentric world has been theorized at least since this time in Alexandria. Aristarchus also predicted that the earth rotates on its axis.

Herophilus is regarded as the father of anatomy for his discoveries about the anatomy of the brain and other organs. Before this, human beings didn't conclusively know what made up their bodies. Theophrastus wrote an eighteen-book history on botany which was a foundational work for the field. These and many other notable intellectuals found a haven in Alexandria where they could collaborate with each other or focus on discovering the intricate design of our physical and intellectual world.

The innovation of this period can be attributed at least to two reasons. First, Alexandria was a prosperous and commercially successful city. It was strategically located in between both Asia and Western Europe and had the ability to accommodate the largest ships of the time. Grains and papyrus were exported all over the Mediterranean, and export of these crops, in addition to regional raw materials made the fortune of Alexandria. It was also a trading port that helped increase prosperity in the region.

With abundant raw material and resources, Ptolemy and his empire could afford mercenary armies to secure and control the military needs of the empire. This also meant that the common man was able to focus his energy on pursuits of the mind, body, and soul. Harlow's hierarchy of needs comes to mind[18]: considering that the common man didn't need to spend his time worrying about his very existence, a lot of mental energy and time was freed up for other pursuits.

With the economic stability and growth that the region offered, the rulers patronized scholars, and their main focus was the increase the knowledge of the world—and with it, wealth and their empire. As we saw during the hundred schools of thought era, and as we look through the later history of our world, patronization of scholars and artists has been a key ingredient in stimulating intellectual, scientific and economic growth.

Second, people from different cultures lived in, grew up or came together under the banner of Alexandria. Different points of view, a keen curiosity for how the world operates, and unorthodox ideas were accepted in this city during the time. No thoughts were too absurd as to demand the exile or the ridicule that we see in some empires before and after this. These ideas had to meet a few criteria, though—they shouldn't directly relate to, or criticize, the political climate or upset the kings (and for what it's worth, shouldn't disrespect cats!)

Alexandria marked the beginning of three centuries of explosion in learning, generation of "alternate" world views and new theories. Not only did science, philosophy, and literature undergo a major revolution during this period, we also saw creation of new gods and a new explanation in the roles they played in human affairs. Some ideas suggested that gods did exist, but were disinterested in human affairs; others suggested that gods were just ancient kings long forgotten; yet other ideas suggested that gods didn't exist at all.

As science started answering questions otherwise attributed to mythology or acts of god, new gods were created still. We were early on in our scientific learning, and perhaps weren't ready to accept that all questions may someday be answerable by observation and hypothesis, and we continued to attribute different theories to acts of god and build faith.

During this period, as it was in the Qin Dynasty, there was continued application of magic, astrology, and other pseudoscience. Magic and pseudoscience existed before our ability to answer some questions scientifically, but it may have perhaps increased our belief in the supernatural when the scientific method was developed: *if we could find new methods to answer questions which were previously unanswerable scientifically, we probably just haven't found the right methods and devices to use, in order to answer questions about our future and our destiny.*

An increase in knowledge and understanding of science should technically give rise to an increase in our beliefs in pseudoscience, religion, theology and the like, even if temporarily. If we question our world view and come to realize that what we had thought about ourselves and our home has been incorrect, why should any of our other beliefs be correct? This may seem counter-intuitive, but over different tests, pseudoscience doesn't stand the test of time.

Perhaps if we tried again, this time, differently, we might realize that we may be able to prove the unprovable. The key difference in science and pseudoscience is that in science we should eventually be able to come to a reasonable, probable answer (or theory). Questioning the entirety of our beliefs—fact-based and faith-based—is important in the wake of new, related information so that we may be sure that we are pursuing the correct and logical course.

Pseudoscience will not stand the test of time and repeated probing in different contexts. Faith-based religion may never be provable. In these cases, the logical courses to take are to accept that our beliefs or theories were either incorrect (which is great because we've now eliminated one or more possibilities and are closer to the answer) or unanswerable (maybe we'll answer them someday, maybe we won't, maybe we'll harbor these beliefs anyway).

We've come a long way in the domain of science and reason, but when we face the unanswerable, we still cling to an orthodox view of attributing the unknown to god with

increasing and definite certitude. We cling to our beliefs with our dear lives, sometime even with increased faith in the face of evidence on the contrary.

Those with power or influence to affect change have an increased need for this understanding. When we can influence, we can change the course of our sphere of influence, of how people think, act, react, and behave. Our sphere of influence is often times larger than we think and is affected in more subtle ways. Educators, heads of organizations or a part thereof, volunteers, consultants, parents, and those in the service industry, among others, all can and do play a part in influencing thought, educating those who will benefit and influencing those who can be influenced.

In these interactions—verbal or otherwise—we have a responsibility to understand what we do not understand but can learn from others, and to educate those we can who may benefit from knowing. Children in schools need to be taught the scientific method, this method of thinking, and accepting or disproving facts can and should be taught at an early age. Chances are, it's a fun way to engage the students even more. But we must first educate ourselves, make our thought processes fail proof and not fall prey to fallacies of thought in the first place, all three of which are not easily accomplished.

When one ideology is encouraged or enforced, and the general population hasn't much freedom of thought and expression, the result of that oppression is stagnation. Not just of culture and of intellect, but of economy as well. This

stagnation comes along with the eventual decline in the empire, nation, community and organization where stagnation is taking place. Throughout different time periods, a lack of progress can be correlated with stagnation and decline.

*

In our world today, social media plays an important role not just as a source of entertainment, but as a source of content, and in some cases, wisdom and knowledge. What we see today is an infinite influx of content, a spinning of the same articles in different ways on different blogs, or an endless series of memes and cats that can entertain us for hours on end. On the other side of the spectrum, there is a curation of knowledge and dispelling of myths at a scale we've never seen before. Sites like Quora and Reddit dispel ancient myths because they are forums where people share their knowledge—and one only need ask the right questions. What we have today is some level of freedom of thought, of sharing, of contradicting one another to find out the true series of events, or at least engage in different points of view.

The other additional beauty of freedom of thought and expression is that disciplines and cultures learn from each other. The developments in one field of study can help another field's progress, and they quite often do. Alexandria was a place that allowed this freedom of thought and expression. The disparate cultures from which scholars and individuals

came to Alexandria perhaps propelled the progress it made.

The Alexandrian library was built scroll by scroll. Every scroll that arrived in Alexandria would be copied, the original kept in the library and a copy was returned to those who brought it. The library was perhaps a curation of all the knowledge in the world, and Alexandria, a curation of different thought processes, viewpoints, races, religions, and fields of study.

But on some level, everything that rises must fall. We see this change everywhere. New technologies make established products and services obsolete. New products effectively disrupt industries, create new jobs while driving others to extinction. The introduction and acceptance of email didn't just coincide with a fall in the usage of old-fashioned snail mail, it was a precursor of the fall. CDs meant floppy disks were obsolete, and USB drives meant CDs went obsolete, and so the cycle continues with cloud technologies. *We* must accept progress or be left behind. Dogma doesn't help our survival, and in cases where we are comfortable enough to hold on to the old, we are effectively holding on to our own destruction.

Destruction, change, and the old paving the way for the new is an age-old truism. Human beings are both creators and destroyers, but not all destruction is *negative*. The first kind occurs out of our sheer need to destruct. The wars we fight, the bombs we drop, and the forests we destroy for no reason but for the sake of destruction or the sake of proving

our superiority. The second kind is the destruction that happens as a result of creation. We create something new, and it replaces or uses the old. Cars are fairly different today than the first cars we created, so are the planes we fly, and so are the clothes we wear. Creating the new means leaving the old in the past, in some cases destroying industries and old ways of life in the process.

Both of these kinds of destruction are a part of our past and our present and the line between the two can sometimes be very blurry, especially when we are the ones who cause the destruction. So it was with Alexandria. The destruction of the library of Alexandria is popularly attributed to three distinct events, but which one of these events is responsible for the most damage is generally debated:

- In 48 BCE by Julius Caesar,
- In the 3rd Century CE by Christian followers, and
- During the Muslim conquest of Egypt in 642 CE.

Depending on the historian retelling the story and his religious or political views, the blame is placed on any of the three events. Some blame the Christians, mentioning that the church was against the use of science and/or reason. Others use a documented quote from the Muslim invaders as a definitive source[19] and use it as a source of pride in their Caliph.

John Hannam, the author of *God's Philosophers*,

does an excellent job of looking at the available documentation around the library. After scrutinizing the disparate sources available from the time and since, he comes to the conclusion that the Royal Library of Alexandria probably did not exist in its original form after Caesar's siege of Alexandria[20].

After two and a half centuries of the library's existence, Julius Caesar's troops, during a siege, seem to have accidentally burned a part of the library. Histories on the life of Caesar note that this error was undone by his successor 7 years later. But various sources from the period and after do not mention any existence of the library at all. That the library may have burned down during the siege of Alexandria by Caesar is not too far-fetched.

It is also probable that the Royal Library may have been moved after these events and existed in some form, in a different location but with the same name. We know of a sister library that existed at the Serapeum in Alexandria. The many mentions to a burning of *a* library at Alexandria could be any of the libraries that existed in Alexandria since.

Edward Gibbon's *"The Decline and Fall of Rome"* is generally seen as an exhaustive history of the Roman Empire, in which he posits that the cause of destruction of the Alexandrian library was Pope Theophilus, a follower of Christianity. Gibbon, certainly a respected historian with regards to the Roman world, was also an open critic of the Christian Church. Given his position on the church, when information presented agreed with his pre-existing views, he probably accepted the first-hand account that mentioned the destruction of "the great library of Alexandria".

In the reading of any facts, we must consider the source of our information. Gibbon's clear anti-Christian views may or may not play a role in his conclusions, but being aware of the position taken by our source gives us a more complete picture of the fact itself.

It is also possible that all these events had some impact on the fall of the city of Alexandria, and consequently, the library. Even if the library was not completely destroyed in one event, we know that it eventually did. It is also interesting to note that no archeological evidence of the library itself is found, which makes the loss even more appalling.

After the destruction of the library, intellectual stimulation didn't come to an end. Libraries, scholarly patronization, and the development of science continued. Ptolemy's influence was not just limited to his reign. It lasted generations and lasts still today. This *allowance* of scientific questioning was beneficial to his empire, to his people, and to us today. Scientific progress helped Ptolemy progress in military technology, and made for good business for the empire's treasure. Even so, we may never have a real and complete account of the library, its destruction, and the loss of knowledge it contained. ∞

Chapter 5

The Roman World

"Fables should be taught as fables, myths as myths, and miracles as poetic fantasies. To teach superstitions as truths is a most terrible thing. The child mind accepts and believes them, and only through great pain and perhaps tragedy can he be in after years relieved of them."—Elbert Hubbard, Biography of Hypatia[21]

A few centuries after Alexander the Great, Ptolemy, and the Alexandrian library, the Romans took over control of majority of the land that was ruled by the Greeks. Intellectual and cultural stimulation continued in certain disciplines—history, law and oration—while philosophy, poetry, and the arts were considered to be worthwhile pastimes. The Early Roman intellectual sphere was heavily influenced by the Greeks, who—while being slaves to the Roman aristocracy—

also acted as an intellectual proxy in architecture, medicine, philosophy and other disciplines that didn't otherwise interest the Romans.

Where people of different faiths coexisted in relative peace in the Greek world, things were a little different under Roman control. Polytheists were a vast majority in the land, and as the Romans conquered more of the Greek world, they didn't impose a religion on their subjects.

The Pagan people would routinely discriminate against monotheistic religions—Judaism and later Christianity. Christianity, for one, had a very rocky relationship with the roman religions. Their secretive rituals didn't help build trust in the Romans, who feared that not worshipping the Roman gods would call for anger, destruction and the eventual fall of their land.

Over the course of the three centuries in the Roman Empire, practicing Christians were generally persecuted due to the secret nature of their rituals and practices. Paganism, on the other hand, a widely accepted and practiced religion during the time, was one that was practiced publicly. Romans were expected to respect their emperors and offer sacrifices to the Pagan gods; the individual and personal belief in God that is popular in modern society today wasn't so common. Faith was more communal than personal.

Christianity came to be first as a sect of Judaism and later developed into its own religion distinct from Judaism by the first century CE. The Jews, who co-existed with Roman

Pagans, were generally tolerated for three reasons: First, their religion was legitimized in the Roman society by their ancestry; second, the Jews had their own rites and rituals, and the pagans understood these rites, and third, the Jews were required to pay the Jewish tax to practice their religion[22]. Christianity, on the other hand, was a relatively new religion, their secret rites, sometimes practiced at night, confused and aroused suspicion in the local Pagan population. Christians also didn't pay the "Jewish tax", which many consider to be the time when Christianity officially became its own religion, rather than a sect of Judaism.

The Pagans of the time detested Christians not only because they didn't understand Christian practices but because they also considered Christian beliefs to affect the society negatively. Practicing Christianity meant that the established Pagan gods would not be worshiped, and they would be angered, leading to imminent disaster. This kind of superstitious thinking was not unusual for the time period, and we see this consistently in many different religions— especially Abrahamic—where people who don't believe in the established gods are considered to be heretics.

What we consider to be superstition was widely accepted to be "true", and gods who overlooked and controlled our world were an integral part of the thought process of the population. To that end, Pagans were willing to stone Christians publicly or ridicule them. Since Roman emperors of the time were expected to ensure stability in their regions, if a rift existed between two groups of different faiths, the emperor or his office intervened.

One Roman Emperor, Constantine is considered to have single-handedly made it possible for Christianity to co-exist with Paganism and Judaism, and later help it flourish. After four centuries of the Roman conquest of the Greek world, Constantine came to power. His life reads like nothing short of a historical action movie, wrought with politics, hostage situations, wars and plots to escape and conquer. He was the son of an innkeeper's Daughter, Helena, and of Constantius, who later ruled the western half of the Roman Empire.

A statue of Constantine, Musée du Capitole, Rome 23

Constantius commanded one of the largest armies in the Roman Empire, and being the son of an emperor gave Constantine certain privileges and a launching pad for his career. Although, his own role in shaping his life is no less extraordinary. Having lived for 65 years, he was an emperor for almost half of his life. He "united" the Roman Empire, put an end to Tetrarchy[24], in which rule was divided among four individuals, and turned it into a hereditary system. He conquered almost all of his adversaries and introduced gold coinage that would be in use for a thousand years after his death, but perhaps most importantly, it was he who made Christianity an accepted religion in the Roman Empire.

Constantine spent his early life in the military, rising through the ranks, proving his efficacy as a warrior and a commander, becoming a respected strategist and eventually being elected as a military tribune[25]. While serving under the Roman Emperor, Diocletian, Constantine fought in wars for half a decade. In Syria, he fought the Persians; in Danube and Mesopotamia, he fought the barbarians. Eventually, he returned to Nicomedia, where he served Diocletian's court and was held as a virtual hostage. His return from the field to Nicomedia coincided with Diocletian's persecution of Christians, the most severe persecution in Roman History.

	East	West
Augustus	Diocletian	Maximian
Caesar	Galerius	Constantius

The tetrarchy, during Diocletian's rule, before 305 CE

Diocletian ordered the church in Nicomedia to be destroyed, Christian scriptures to be burnt and stripped Christians from official ranks. Christian priests were prosecuted. There were only two other major persecutions of

Christians before Diocletian's—by the emperor Nero in the early Roman Empire (64 AD), and an empire-wide persecution in the third century[26]. There were ad-hoc edicts against Christians but these were generally preceded by an agitated public. Generally, there was no motivation for Roman emperors to prosecute Christians except to mitigate chaos and civil unrest.

For a relatively young man who interacted with intellectuals in both Pagan and Christian circles, this must have affected him deeply. Constantine is said to have neither taken part in the prosecutions nor oppose them at the time, though in his later writings, he portrayed himself as a supporter of the Christians. Constantine's experience at this time is vitally important: this may have driven Constantine towards Christianity in his later years, or at the very least given him a reason to side with the Christians: his guilt for his inability to do anything for them. We tend to dehumanize historical figures to the point where their heroism is emotionally invulnerable. On the contrary, many of the accomplishments of major historical figures can be attributed to their passion and need to prove and do something – for themselves and for others.

Diocletian was to live for only a few more years after Constantine returned to Nicomedia, during which time, one of Diocletian's co-emperors, Galerius, positioned himself strategically to take over the rule from Diocletian[27]. Under the tetrarchy, rule was divided among four individuals: Two

Augusti, a title given to senior emperors, and two Caesars, a title given to junior emperors. The Roman Empire was divided into the east and the west regions, with one Augustus and one Caesar ruling each region. The general population expected Constantine to be named one of the four emperors after Diocletian's resignation—but events didn't turn out so. Diocletian named Constantius the Augustus in the west, and Galerius the Augustus in the east.

	East	West
Augustus	Galerius	Constantius
Caesar	Severus	Maximinus

The tetrarchy, after Diocletian's resignation, after 305 CE

Once Galerius was in power, Constantine realized the imminent danger he was in if he remained in Galerius' court. Some sources detail that Constantine was required to enter into a one-on-one combat with a lion, and in another situation, he was forced to lead a team through a swamp in the Danube River. One particularly engaging story revolves around Constantine's escape from Galerius' court, where Constantine got Galerius drunk, and fled:

> *"In 305, Diocletian decided it was time for him and a reluctant Maximian to abdicate. Constantius became the Western Augustus, while Galerius became the Eastern Augustus. Because his*

father was now Augustus, many expected Constantine to become his successor. But the Tetrarchy was not hereditary by nature. Instead, Galerius, who had greater power, appointed his partisans, Severus and Maximinus II Daia, as the new Caesars.

This turn of events left Constantine humiliated. Coming to the obvious conclusion that he had little future at the court of Galerius, Constantine began to look for a pretext to escape. Constantius, probably aware of his son's predicament, sent a letter to Galerius requesting Constantine's aid in Britain.

Propaganda suggests that Constantine secured the approval of Galerius after a heavy night of drinking. Then, without waiting for Galerius to change his mind, Constantine fled that very night. Due to the danger of being caught, he hamstrung the horses at every post-house he passed."[28]

Once Constantine reached the west, where his father had jurisdiction, his life turned around, and Constantine was in greater control of his destiny. Within a year of Constantine's arrival, Constantius took to illness and passed on the empire to Constantine—who would only accept his new title if the military agreed. And they did. At the time, Constantius was the emperor of Britain, Spain, and Gaul[29] which he bequeathed to Constantine.

Constantius generally had a more tolerant policy towards Christians, and their persecutions in the west were less severe than in the east. Following in his father's footsteps, Constantine ended the persecution of Christians and saw it as a sensible way to distinguish himself from Galerius.

If it wasn't for the events at Nicomedia and the subsequent challenges Constantine went through to become Emperor, the course of Christian—and human—history may have been quite different.

During his early years, Constantine was able to move in both Christian and Pagan circles, and for the most part of his early career, did not take a side on either religion. In fact, he was baptized only towards the end of his life, even though he favored and fought for Christianity during most of the time he was an emperor.

Constantine's trials did not end when he took over his rule. He not only had to prove himself as a legitimate heir to his father's share of the Roman Empire but also deal with three other emperors who were unhappy with the events leading up to Constantine's emperorship.

In a few years, Constantine conquered the western empire and united it. He used Christian symbology quite extensively, perhaps as a tool to unite his people, to undo the guilt inflicted by his inability to protect the Christian people during Diocletian's persecution, or by a sheer need to find meaning through religion.

By the end of Constantine's rule, Christianity was well established in the Roman Empire. Paganism, by this point, although co-existed with other religions, had come to be thought of as an inferior religion, with "Pagan" being used as an insult. Tables had turned. Monotheistic religions were generally considered to be more powerful than their polytheistic counterparts and although pagan temples were not yet burned by this time, though they later were, and the Pagans were not yet humiliated publicly, the seeds were sowed when Christianity had become accepted as the religion of Constantine, the emperor of Rome.

While Constantine certainly did a lot for both the Romans and for Christianity, from the perspective of our knowledge, we are left with a less than real account of his life and rule. Much of what survives of Constantine's life was rewritten after his conquest of his adversaries. Most writings paint him as a paragon of virtue and *the* standard by which a ruler ought to measure his efficacy. Rewriting history to favor the current rule is not a new phenomenon. We saw this during Qin Shi Huang's rule in China almost 600 years before Constantine, and countless others since, where "history" was rewritten to suit those who had the ability to wield influence over it.

While rewriting of texts may be motivated by personal or communal ambitions, or ego, we—the readers of history—and those in our future, are left with only a partially true account of the events that occurred, at best. We lose some valuable knowledge and understanding in the process.

The loss of our knowledge occurs in at least three different cases: When history, writings, art, artifacts and the like are intentionally destroyed; when these are re-written or overwritten; or when they're lost to time. The first two are intentional, but the third is a tragedy we have no control over. Information can be lost to time naturally, or anatomically. There are natural corrosions of objects that hold ideas, knowledge, and thoughts of people, but when an idea that could spark inspiration for the next few generation is forgotten, it is our own anatomy betraying us—what a pity. We can't do anything but wait for the next moment of inspiration that sparks the same idea.

The destruction that we do have control over, is still prevalent and often times repeated throughout our history. Constantine certainly made it possible for Christianity to flourish in the Roman world while also rewriting how he was perceived and remembered by future generations.

*

Christians of the time generally believed (and still do) that the omnipotent, omniscient God, was composed of three distinct entities which made up the one God. These three entities were the Father, The Son, and the Holy Spirit. This was a major distinction between Judaism, (of which Christianity was originally a sect) Islam, and Christianity. If god was further divisible, then it was not the same Abrahamic

God that the other two major religions believed in. So what were the three parts that made up the Christian God?

God the Father: The first person in the Holy Trinity, Father and creator of the universe. Also the father of Jesus Christ.

God the Son: The second person in the Holy Trinity, intrinsically the same as God the Father, but distinct in personality. Jesus Christ is the metaphysical embodiment of God the Son. Pre-existed before the universe was created, and is co-eternal with God the Father and the Holy Spirit.

The Holy Spirit: The Third Person in the Holy Trinity. In the Nicene Creed[30], The Holy Spirit is referred to as "The Lord, The Giver of Life". It can be thought of as the force that animates living creatures, among other things.

In Christian theology, these three parts of the one God is the Holy Trinity. Each of the three persons that make up God co-exist and are co-eternal; they existed before the universe was created and will exist after the world ends.

Arius, a Presbyterian priest from Alexandria, concluded that God the Son was created by the Father at some point in time, and was therefore subordinate to God the

Father, and did not pre-exist in the universe before it was created. We can see why such a conclusion would offend the church and create discord among the Christians of the time: it is one of the core philosophies of Christianity that the three parts of the trinity are co-eternal, co-exist, and three parts of the One. This was a direct attack on the Christian God; it was considered heresy.

The idea of God the Son being created by the Father, and therefore being subservient to the Father had spread across the Roman world by this time and was a matter of disturbance to the stability of the Church. Since Christianity was legalized, the Christian church had gained power in the Roman world. Constantine, who helped legalize Christianity, and helped it get to the point where it was, was now directly involved in resolving this dispute.

Three hundred Christian representatives from different parts of the Roman Empire were called for, to *"listen to the impartial exhortation of [their] fellow-servant"* and put an end to the dispute. It is said that after two months of discussions, the majority was on the side of Trinitarians: that is, the Son was not created by God the Father but exists independently of this world and is essentially of the same substance as God the Father ("con-substantial").

After the gathering of all the Christian representatives ("The Council of Nicea"), only two of the three hundred representatives didn't sign the creed that condemned the teachings of Arius. Constantine and the Church deemed the matter resolved and ordered punishment by death to anyone who wouldn't surrender Arian writings to be burned.

> *"In addition, if any writing composed by Arius should be found, it should be handed over to the flames, so that not only will the wickedness of his teaching be obliterated, but nothing will be left even to remind anyone of him. And I hereby make a public order, that if someone should be discovered to have hidden a writing composed by Arius, and not to have immediately brought it forward and destroyed it by fire, his penalty shall be death. As soon as he is discovered in this offense, he shall be submitted for capital punishment....."*

This is the second historical record we have of mass burnings of books, the first one being during the Hundred Schools of Thought era. More significantly, Constantine, who was famed for his making it possible for Christianity to co-exist with other religions, issued an edict to burn the writings of a Christian.

We have very few records of what Arius actually taught. Except for the quotes used in critical commentary against Arianism, we have no information on the teachings and the motivations of Arius. Almost all of the documentation that supported Arianism was burned, and all that was left was in the form of quotes used by his critics to impale him.

The burning of his books and philosophies, however, was not the end of Nontrinitarianism. Throughout the ages, different groups of Christians have generally come to accept that God the Son was created by God the Father, rather than being *consubstantial*. Mormons and Jehovah's Witnesses are both contemporary examples of groups that believe in Nontrinitarianism.

A couple of things stand out here. First, the theory of the three parts of the Holy Trinity was created conceptually and over time. Some Christians believe in varying ideas of the concept. So even within Christianity, there is very little proof, except for one's belief in the concepts, of what is the true nature of "god", if there is any. Further, if the concept of the trinity was invented sometime in the 1st century AD, only two things are possible: Either man didn't know and understand the trinity before this, or it was an intellectual and theological development based on questions that needed to be answered regarding the nature of god.

Which one of these is true really depends on the strength of one's belief and the position one takes for and against religion. To some extent, it is worth mentioning that this is true of most religions: That the intellectual concepts were developed over time, canonized, and eventually came to be believed as the "word of god".

Throughout our history, we have assigned divinity to people, idols, concepts, or beliefs at different times and in different contexts. If god truly is above our understanding, then all we can do is *try* to understand him/her/it. Assigning a divinity to something above our understanding is either disrespectful, or is unnecessary to a god we cannot comprehend, let alone committing violence and propagating destruction in the names of those who created us.

But this also raises an interesting question: who are we to grant divinity to god or a part thereof? If we are his creation, it doesn't matter whether we think he is divine or not. Is it our arrogance and self-importance that leads us to believe that this divinity is ours to assign? Wouldn't divinity be an external, observable trait—something we can observe and apply to the trinity or any parts thereof?

Either way, it is truly fascinating when we find things in places we don't expect. Those who oppose an idea actually help propagate it further. Agriculturism from the Hundred Schools of Thought Era in China suffered a similar fate as the books of Arius, and lived on as a legacy similarly. All texts relating to the subjects were burned, but we know about Agriculturism and Arianism today only because it faced fierce opposition during the time. If it wasn't for that recorded critical opposition, with the burning of the texts, there would be very little—if any—information passed on to us from the time, and the loss would truly be ours: we wouldn't even know that something like Agriculturism, like Nontrinitarianism existed.

As Christianity developed and spread throughout Europe, its sphere of influence grew. It not only influenced, but shaped, the world in which we live. The idea of an omnipotent and omniscient god, of the separation of church and state, of universities, of science, of capitalism all find their roots in the Christian influence of our world.

Christianity has had a profound effect in the development of our world, with missionaries over the course of the centuries trotting the globe looking to convert followers. Some of the first universities—Oxford, Cambridge, St. Andrews, Edinburgh—were founded as Christian universities. Scientific inquiry and the protection of our ancient Greek knowledge, were enabled by the Christian priests who made it their life's work to understand how the world their God created operated.

Which brings us to a fairly widespread belief of the "dark ages" and the position of the church against science. After all, we have stories of this suppression: Galileo was exiled, and his theory of a heliocentric model of universe wasn't accepted; Giordano Bruno, a martyr of science, was burned for heresy for his acceptance of Copernican system of astronomy; the Inquisitions and their resulting deaths.

Scholars today debunk the real existence of any dark age during the middle ages. The myth of little to no scientific progress and a suppression of reason is widespread, propagated by anti-Christians, scientists, and writers during and after the Renaissance period.

After the fall of Rome and the resulting decline in literacy and organization of knowledge, Christian monks actually had a major part to play in preserving classical knowledge that would otherwise be lost to the wars and the instability of the time[31]. Much of the Christianity's stand on science has been to understand the world God has created, and through it, to understand the God who created this world. By understanding the inner workings of the world, one may understand its creator.

Today, Atheism is a more widely accepted way of life, but prior to this modern world, and the development that science has brought with it, religion and science went relatively hand in hand. Over the course of Christian history, we see various positions taken by people of different backgrounds: some say that Christianity (or faith and religion in general) and science are incompatible, while others maintain that religion and science are two sides of the same coin.

It is much easier, in general, to look at certain events and conclude the position a religion takes with regards to god or science. In reality, this is a complicated relationship. Men of the Christian faith—both who believe in religion strongly and those who were merely born into it—routinely have made stellar progress in science. Kepler, Descartes, Newton, Aquinas, even Bruno and Galileo were Christians.

We could point at the expulsion of Galileo or the burning of books of Arians, or the official banned books by the Christian Church and easily, though incorrectly, say that the Christian position is that of opposition to science. This would be lazy and incorrect. Without what was the Christian world after the fall of Rome, much of the ancient works may not be available to us today which were preserved by Irish Christian monks [32] . Christian scholars helped translate much of scientific and philosophic Greek texts into Arabic at the House of Wisdom, a center of knowledge during the Islamic Golden Age.

But even so, we must be careful not to remove the human equation from conversations about history. With every intellectual and scientific innovation, as new thoughts pave way for new ways of thinking, established organizations and influential individuals feel threatened and act from a place of fear. In looking at the history of mankind, this behavior is not hard to see.

Let's take for instance the story of Hypatia, one of the earliest women aligned with science[33] and a mathematician of note in ancient Alexandria. Her story is used quite extensively in Anti-Christian conversations—suggesting that a mob of Christians killed her for her anti-Christian views. According to historical accounts of the time, it is more likely that her death was politically motivated—where two individuals of power in the Alexandrian world couldn't reconcile their views and where Hypatia became the central point of contention.

Depending on the account one reads, one can find ample distortion of historical events. The events, as we see later in this book, depend on the frame one is presenting the story from. Communities of people, individuals who want to present Christianity in a negative light portray that Hypatia was killed by a Christian mob. This version of the story is technically true but incomplete.

This is not an argument in defense of the church, or in defense of the people who commit the acts. On the contrary, in looking back at history—we can see that faith, beliefs, identity may be a tool, used time and again, by individuals to destroy or distort. They can be used to destroy: my faith versus your faith; my beliefs versus yours. They can be used to distort: He did so because he is a Christian, or a Mexican or White, or Black or Brown.

One way to reconcile some of the acts of humans are to apply them directly to those who did them: Whether a Christian, Muslim, Hindu or Atheist wages war, war is war. If he destroys, regardless of his background, destruction is destruction. But we, as humans, must question ourselves in what we believe constantly. If what we stand for, what we believe in—our country, religion, community—has the power and influence over this world, and that power and influence is used to destroy and ridicule and demoralize, we ought to ask ourselves if our beliefs align with those of our communities.

We live in a world where disruptions are everywhere. The Ubers of the world ensure the disruption of the old taxi companies, the Netflixes of the world guarantee the extinction of home video stores. The convenience of applying these new technologies in our lives is easy to see. The adoption of these technologies is on the basis of the perceived value it brings to our lives. Why must our belief in religion and science not be the same? Why mustn't we, when provided with evidence, old or new, change our points of view to align with what is true or probable?

Although controversial, we must understand that theology, scripture, belief is created by man. There was a time when the things we now believe in didn't exist, and there will be a time in the future when they won't. That along with us, our beliefs are also temporal. Is it more valuable to cling to dogma than to be open-minded? Is it more wondrous to let the mysteries of nature unfold through inquiry than to believe that everything has only one explanation—one God and one story of our coming to existence? ∞

Chapter 6

In The Heart of India

"Grief can be the garden of compassion. If you keep your heart open through everything, your pain can become your greatest ally in your life's search for love and wisdom."—Rumi

Over the course of their respective histories, the eastern and the western world developed quite differently. Each region developed its religions, values, philosophies, material wealth, depending on what each of the societies deemed to be important. But they didn't develop in a total vacuum. The east and the west have been known to be connected as far back as the second millennium BCE through a trade route called the Silk Road. Trade of gemstones, artworks, and horses already took place much before many of the empires, dynasties and kingdoms mentioned here even came into existence. Lying in between the east and the west, on the Silk Road, was the Indian Subcontinent. The philosophies of this region, lying in the center of the two disparate worlds, developed differently still.

On one of these routes, in the heart of India, was founded a treasure trove of knowledge. Nalanda, one of the oldest teaching institutions in the world, was a Buddhist monastery that grew over the course of seven centuries from 500 CE to 1200 CE. Religious practice at Nalanda, and indeed the region, was not limited to a deep understanding of religious literature only. Monks who lived in the monastery were learned in a wide range of subjects from grammar to logic to Buddhism; the library consisted of large volumes of books in subjects like astronomy, logic, grammar, astrology, literature, and medicine[34].

Growing from a flourishing village on a major trade route in Central India to harboring one of the world's oldest and largest institutions, Nalanda was, at its peak about 12 hectares, or the equivalent of 30 football fields. Nalanda grew to become one of the largest ancient systematic teaching institutions in the world, following the formalized methods learned from the Vedas.

Almost 500 years before the first Christian university, Nalanda was founded. This kind of a teaching system was possible because of the secularity that was promoted by the Gupta Empire, which ruled a majority of the Indian subcontinent for a little more than three centuries leading up to the founding of the university. While the kings of the Gupta regime followed Hinduism, they patronized other contemporary religions as well—Buddhism and Jainism.

Outside of the patronization of the different religions, scholars and works that focused on science, astronomy, engineering and arts were supported. In many cases, these were not mutually exclusive: Patronizing religion meant patronizing science since many of the religious monks took it upon them to understand the physical and metaphysical world. The three-century rule of the Gupta Empire is referred to as the Golden Age of India, and for no small reason. Many unprecedented scientific, artistic and literary innovations took place over the course of the three-century rule of the Guptas.

In the field of literature, this period gave us the Kama sutra. Kama Sutra is a work that is now synonymous with creative sexual positions, and was written during this period by Vastyayana. Contrary to popular belief, it is not merely a book that contains 64 different sexual positions, but actually entails an explanation of the nature of love. It acts as a guide to living a graceful and virtuous life. Kama translates to desire, which is considered to be one of the four goals of a Hindu life, the other three being artha (prosperity and wealth), dharma (righteousness, though often misconstrued as *religion),* and moksha (liberation from the world of karma). And Sutra can be loosely translated into a "manual". Kama sutra, then, can be translated to a manual of desires.

Another poet of the time, Kalidasa, who remained

influential in Europe till the 19th century, flourished during this period. Kalidasa's works inspired such figures as Rabindranath Tagore, an influential figure in the Indian independence and a Bengali-Indian Polymath, Sir William Osler, father of modern medicine, and Johann Wolfgang Von Goethe, known for his literary works and scientific treatises. Perhaps the most interesting aspect of Kalidasa is his study of the romantic and erotic nature of literature, through the concept of *Shringara*. *Shringara* is the emotion generated as a result of the love between and a woman. The perpetually colorful movie industry of India—Bollywood—remains the herald of *Shringara*, and perhaps owes its inspiration to Kalidasa.

Kalidasa writes also about the nine scholars that formed the court of Chandragupta II. He says that literary and scientific innovation in the time was possible because of the consortium of these nine scholars in the Royal court of this Gupta king. It is generally contested that these nine scholars called Navratna (Nine crown jewels) didn't live and flourish at the same time, and therefore couldn't have formed the court of the King. It is possible, however, that these scholars lived at different times but flourished due to the patronization of Royalty.

There were outstanding innovations in the sciences as well: Aryabhata, a mathematician and astronomer, is said to have lived and flourished towards the end of the Gupta Empire. He created a working approximation of the number pi; postulated that the earth rotates on its axis, in contrast to the popular contemporary view that the sky rotated and the earth stood still; scientifically explained that the moon and other planets reflect sunlight, while the prevailing explanations of the time were mythological driven; and he was the first Indian mathematician to calculate the circumference of the earth almost accurately. He touched upon, very primitively, the idea of gravity, explaining why objects do not fall out of the earth. Perhaps most importantly, he invented the concept of the decimal positional system[35] and envisioned the concept of zero[36].

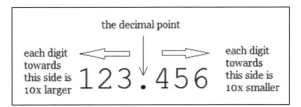

The decimal positional system. This may not sound like a massive invention today because of its ubiquity, but for almost 4000 years of human history, we didn't have this system.

In the west, the idea of "nothing" was brought forward by Democritus almost 8 centuries before this in a completely different context. A quote widely attributed to him goes thus: "Nothing exists except atoms and empty space; everything else is opinion." Democritus is one of the earliest persons who believed there to be "an indivisible particle" that we have a record of. The other aspect of his theory was that "empty space" exists. His contemporaries, and indeed those who succeeded him—including Aristotle—believed that empty space—nothingness—cannot exist. If it exists, it's not empty or "nothing".

Everything we saw around us had some properties associated with it, so nothingness wasn't really a possibility we'd thought of. Up until this point in our history, even if nothing *could* conceptually exist, logically, we couldn't fathom it. In many early western cultures, especially as the philosophies developed, reason was believed to be of the utmost importance, and through reasoning, man *could* understand the different aspects of the world. As our sciences progressed, we came to the conclusion, that there must exist things in our dimension that we cannot see, feel or sense.

The discovery of infrared lights, gravity (theorized), atoms, radio waves are all things that we could only fathom or imagine; things that eluded us for the simple reason that our senses are not acute enough to observe these things. In contrast, an intrinsic feature of the Hindu, Buddhist and Jain religions is the idea of the Absolute void and the belief that things exist beyond the human senses.

Logically this thought makes sense, *nothing* cannot *exist*. If it is *nothing* then it cannot be in existence in our world. Therefore, everything in our world exists, including nothing. Our intellectual and linguistic limitations sometimes hinder our ability to see through paradoxes created by our language[37].

Conceptually, *zero*—the number and nothingness—does exist. The Europeans learned of the number from the Arabs, and the Arabs, in turn, learned of this from the Indians. Hence "numbers" are called Arabic by the Europeans, while Arabic scholars called these the *Hindu* numerals. In mathematics, the invention and the utility of the number zero was of course, nothing short of, revolutionary. It enabled Descartes to create his Cartesian co-ordinate system (the ubiquitous x- and y-axis charts that we use) and paved the way for calculus, which propelled our world into the industrial revolution. It was this zero that is responsible for our technological, economical, engineering, financial and scientific advancement. So much for *nothing*.

During the Gupta rule, the healthcare systems were subject to some innovations, too. A form of alternative medicine, whose origins can be traced back to 5000 BCE[38], is the Ayurveda. One of the three main written records of the text on medicine and surgery survives from this period. Visitors from China speak of the healthcare system of the empire, the approach to medicine and texts on how medical clinics should be equipped.

It is thoroughly unfortunate that no biographies exist of many of these authors, including many of the nine scholars, Kalidasa and Vastyayana. This loss is truly ours. In autobiographies and biographies, we may have had the chance to learn about so many different aspects of the lives of scholars and scientists of the time, and their social and intellectual motivations to further their fields of study. In looking back at Indian history, many of our records—of people *and* the subjects they wrote about—are incomplete. Complete records of history and correct attribution of many of these inventions has been a challenge in Indian history. Take, for instance, Kalidasa. It is contested that Kalidasa was not one individual, but four different individuals by the same name. And works that are passed onto us may be attributed to anyone of them. Where in the other cultures, biographies were repurposed to make a man seem more virtuous or the like, in India, we have a lack of written biographies.

Western scholarship certainly has helped in opening up India to the world, but certain nuances in the religion can only be understood, and perhaps communicated correctly, by Indians. Hinduism—for instance—is not a *religion*, per se. Many Indian texts are considered fluid to the point where historically, many people have contributed and expanded texts over time. An accurate scholarship and documentation of these is immensely necessary for our progeny to have a fair account of Indian contributions to the world history.

*

As the Gupta Empire faltered after the death of Chandragupta II and his sons, India became increasingly regionalized, and many different kingdoms succeeded the Guptas. One of these was the Pala Dynasty, which patronized Buddhism almost exclusively, though other religions coexisted in their dynasty. Up until the seventh century AD, the religions were supported fairly equally by their patrons, generally wealthy merchants, and royalty. Their patronage could be through building temples, monasteries, land grants and religious monuments. This changed with the Pala dynasty, with Buddhism being exclusively patronized by the royalty.

Nalanda was perhaps the epitome of the cultural, artistic and intellectual innovations that took place in India for three centuries from the fourth to the seventh century CE. The news of the existence of a university at Nalanda reached the Chinese and the Tibetan peoples, among others, students and scholars from these cultures came to Nalanda to learn of its Buddhist and Sanskrit practices. Yijing, a Chinese scholar, is said to have spent ten years at Nalanda, learning of the Buddhist ways.

Nalanda reached new heights under the Palas, and other learning centers were established and modeled after Nalanda, the largest of which was Vikramashila. It is clear that the influence of Nalanda reached far beyond its local geography, but it is unfortunate, however, that we have no local records of what life at Nalanda was like. The writings and translation of the travelling monks and excavations of the region are the only surviving records of how Nalanda was built, what the contents of its library were, and how people and monks interacted and lived in the university. Two Chinese visitors took back with them about 1000 Buddhist and Sanskrit texts from Nalanda in total, which were later translated, and are the major sources of information about the social and architectural structure of the university. They also wrote extensively about their journeys which shed light to the ancient university and how it was built and operated. Yijing writes one account of how the administrative tasks were undertaken by the monks and the peace that prevailed within the university walls:

> *"If the monks had some business, they would assemble to discuss the matter. Then they ordered the officer, Vihārpāl, to circulate and report the matter to the resident monks one by one with folded hands. With the objection of a single monk, it would not pass. ... In case a monk did something without consent of all the residents, he would be forced to leave the monastery. If there was a difference of opinion on a certain issue, they would give reason to convince (the other group). No force or coercion was used to convince."39*

Peace within the society is one thing, but external forces also play a part in the success and continuity of a community. This internal peace alone was not enough to sustain Nalanda for another seven centuries. Around late 12th century CE, Turkish invaders destroyed the university and its surrounding areas and plundered it for what was available for them to take. The libraries were burned in the process, and the university operated in a makeshift fashion for some time as a former shadow of itself. The contents of the library were destroyed, and the monks who lived in the university were slain.

"From 986 CE, the Muslim Turks started raiding northwest India from Afghanistan, plundering western India early in the eleventh century. Force conversions to Islam were made, and Buddhist images smashed, due to the Islamic dislike of idolatry. Indeed in India, the Islamic term for an 'idol' became 'budd'".[40]

An imagining of the ransacking of Nalanda [41]

What happened at Nalanda is an anecdote of what took place towards and after the tenth century in northwest India. The destruction of the university and the knowledge it contained is perhaps symbolic of what happened to Buddhism at large. Largely following a Buddhist practice, the region in which Nalanda was, was still one of the few centers of Buddhism, and with the attack of the Turks, Buddhist monks fled further eastward and to the south of India, effectively wiping out the religion from the country.

*

Though primarily Buddhist, Nalanda's teaching methods were based on the ancient Vedic system. These Vedas were a set of organized texts passed through the generations orally for a millennia until they were redacted sometime in the middle of the 1st millennium BCE. The Vedas formed the basis of Hinduism, and although such shramanic traditions as Buddhism and Jainism actively rejected the Vedas, the concepts discussed in these texts—theology, philosophy, rituals, sacrifices, and mythology—were adopted, developed and discussed in these traditions as well.

Buddhism and Jainism, called the shramanic traditions for their rejection of the Vedas, found their fundamental grounding in some of the other concepts propagated by Hinduism as well: the ideas of Karma, Rebirths, and *liberation* from this world, for instance. While these "unorthodox" traditions were founded around 500 BCE,

Hinduism found its roots almost 1000 years before [42] . Throughout this thousand-year development period, each succeeding generation added to these teachings and transmitted them further orally. These texts eventually culminated into what were called the *Vedas* and were considered to be "authorless" and "not written by any man or superhuman", constituting the sacred texts of Hinduism. These Vedas do not define Hinduism or any religion of the sort per se. They purport to be texts that convey the truth as it is seen in the world.

No such thing as the "religion" of Hinduism really exists, though sects of Hinduism that believe in supreme beings may be called religions. Hinduism is a synthesized philosophy of the many different beliefs, cultures, and traditions, often times internally contradictory, perhaps owing to its characteristic of having no author, no prophet, and no one god. This dualistic, contradictory, way of life may be considered practical because of its subjectivity. What applies to an individual may not apply to another, and the Vedas or the concepts of Hinduism may not apply to an individual in their totality.

Hindus can choose to be polytheistic, monotheistic, pantheistic, humanistic, monistic, agnostic, atheistic, or a combination of them. For instance, in many temples, one would see Ganesha (A God who removes obstacles) and Laxmi (The Goddess of wealth), among other deities, even though a certain sect of Hinduism may consider itself monotheistic.

A depiction of the lord Ganesha[43]. Each group of believers may design the god differently, depending on the local traditions. Though there will exist some similarities among the traditions.

In contrast, Jainism actively rejects that a being created the world—and us with it. In fact, the Jain cosmos is eternal and is neither created nor destroyed. Some of the concepts that the Jain universe promotes are truly remarkable in their thinking, especially for the time period. The Jain universe consists of six eternal substances: the soul (which every living thing has) and five substances that have no soul (space, time, matter, motion, and non-motion). The central tenets of Jainism are threefold:

- **Non-violence:** Intentionally harming any kind of living being is not acceptable except in self-defense. This view is famously adopted by Mahatma Gandhi, who was a major player in the Indian Independence.

- **Non-absolutism:** No viewpoint is absolutely perfect—all points of view are only partially complete because our senses do not grant us a complete understanding of this world. This non-absolutist view of our world is something that is widely accepted in the scientific community today—the fact that we don't know everything is the basis of our quest for knowledge[44].

- **Non-attachment:** This is the idea that in order to reduce suffering, man should not only remove his attachment to material possessions, but also to psychological concepts such as ego and greed.

What is additionally fascinating, perhaps, is that the philosophies of all three of these traditions—Hinduism, Buddhism, and Jainism—were not forced upon their followers. A monk must absolutely abide by asceticism, but those in the society living a normal life were expected to follow as much as their practical life allowed them. There were no belief systems forced upon the followers, at least from a scriptural point of view.

*

On the one hand, it is poetic to believe that these are

the ideals men should live by; on the other, it's naive to imagine that non-violent and peaceful civilizations can succeed in an increasingly material world where conquest through force is constant. Notwithstanding external threats, even the internal makeup of the Ancient Indian society bred contempt and violence. Monks had a tough time during this period—in order to keep followers interested and to spread and grow their religion, over the course of the centuries, priests and scholars needed to find creative ways to adapt to the changing landscape.

During the course of the Indian history, Buddhism, Jainism, and Hinduism saw interesting interactions in their philosophies. These contemporary philosophies were rewritten, repurposed or built upon to gain more followers and support, and to ensure the continuity of the religion. In some cases, to innovate, scriptures were expanded to include references to other religions. In one excerpt of Jainism, Krishna, a god of the Hindu tradition was supposedly made a reincarnation of a Jain follower.

In other cases, Jains directly attacked the opulence and unethical behavior of Hindu Gods—Lord Krishna had multiple wives as a god-king, Shiva was easily angered and beheaded his own son Ganesha; he, a god, also had an extra-marital affair. The motivation behind expansion in scriptures is sometimes straightforward—to gain followers either through putting down another religion, or to make a religion seem more virtuous—and at other times motivated by the elitist nature of the priests—Buddha is supposed to have explicitly directed to not translate Buddhist texts to Sanskrit, but write them in the local languages so they may be accessible to the local populace.

In contrast, the Hindus depended on the priests to mediate an understanding of the *Vedas*, which eventually was mired with ritualistic practices rather than an innate understanding of the texts. Sanskrit was used by the Hindu priests and was inaccessible to the local population, making the priests powerful, but making them "messengers of god". The necessary questioning of the authority was lost as the authority of the translation of these texts were given over to the priests.

This kind of contempt still exists today, not just within India, but globally across different religions. While nationalism unites people based on our national affiliation and pits us against one another, sectarianism ensures that internal conflict prevails.

*

Hinduism and Buddhism today make up the world's third and fourth largest religions. Jainism, however, has had a steady decline, with about four million followers worldwide as of 2011.

Nalanda is today regarded as a UNESCO world heritage site. In 2014, Nalanda University was re-established with the view to commemorate its history, with an expected cost of US$1 billion. As of this writing, close to $12 million dollars were raised with majority of its funding coming from private individuals in Singapore. ∞

Chapter 7

The Contemporary Burnings

"The only thing more painful than learning from experience is not learning from experience." –Anon.

Through the ages, we've shown our power through destruction, and through creation. We've created and destroyed ideas, books, libraries, pieces of art, monuments, forts, people and their communities, and perhaps everything that ever existed. To ensure stability of our worlds, we've exiled those who pose a threat to the stability of society or worse, oppressed them. This is not an exclusive trait belonging to humans who came before us: it seems to be a recurring theme, even in our society today in what seems to us to be the golden age of information and knowledge.

In February 2015, ISIS (later renamed the Islamic State, or IS) burnt through a library and its surrounding areas in Mosul, Northern Iraq, burning over a hundred thousand rare manuscripts. Generations of knowledge and a physical manifestation of our culture was destroyed—in its original form—along with the destruction of these libraries and museums.

The effect of this is probably very different from the effect of book burnings of the past twenty centuries. We now have a larger network to store and share knowledge. Technology has not only enabled us to share information across the solar system but also replicate it with relative ease. In a mere nineteen years, we now know exactly what Pluto looks like, when two decades ago we could only estimate a blurry image of the dwarf planet. NASA's satellite New Horizons sends us pictures of the dwarf planet with an amazing clarity at a distance of 7.5 billion kilometers within a few months.

The knowledge we've gathered in four millennia helps us create technology that makes our lives simpler in almost every respect. It also helps us find ways in which we can help it survive and store it for progeny. With economies globalizing, our knowledge, our wisdom and if not the physical forms of statues and artifacts, their photographic and artistic renditions, are effectively replicated globally.

Our hope, of course, is that these manuscripts, renditions of art and artifacts, were shared and allowed to be online so that they may live on for future generations. Events that threaten to destroy our havens of knowledge today—even if only in the physical world—bring us back to the infancy of our knowledge gathering. All the knowledge in this world doesn't equate to the wisdom we could gain from reflection on history.

We have been committing such atrocities to our culture and our past for the sake of beliefs for millennia. The destruction in Mosul was not an isolated or a superficial incident: The Islamic State does not just want to terrorize people and subjugate them into believing in their version of Islamic philosophies. What the IS wants is to create a new geographical boundary which follows the Quranic writings in its original literal form as it was written in the early seventh century: anything but the absolute, literal interpretation of the Quran is blasphemy and not Islam in its true sense. The Islamic state wants to create what is called a Caliphate—a region ruled over by an Islamic leader called "Caliph"—that enforces the word of Quran and takes measures to ensure its effectiveness.

Non-believers, in the interpretation of the IS, are not just people who do not believe in Islam. Non-believers are all human beings who do not accept, practice and enforce the teachings of Quran literally. There are a few exceptions: Non-Islamic followers can practice their religion by paying a tax ("*Jizya*"), but Muslims who don't literally apply the word of the Quran are heretics.

This raises a question: how literally can we take anything written? Literature is a product of its environment and needs to be read with an understanding of the period in which it was written. With time, all literature grew to make sense of the newfound understanding of the world. The word of god in any religion has developed over time until it was canonized. As man questioned, understood and answered— these answers built the treasure chest of what we so proudly claim to be our beliefs.

In our world, we wouldn't expect a truly learned and/or compassionate member of our society to write with xenophobic undertones or suggest the public stoning of heretics. There are themes universal to human beings across time and space—suffering, longing, pursuit of happiness, passion and the like—but no work can encompass the totality of the human experience, let alone predict the future and suggest that one way to live is the absolute best.

For years Aristotle's work was considered to be the most exhaustive work in philosophy, logic, biology, chemistry, physics, and metaphysics, among others. Much of the western world, for close to two thousand years, took for granted that Aristotle couldn't be wrong. He came to his conclusions based on what he could observe and deduce and concluded that things are the way they are. As the first polymath that we know of in history, the corpus of his work is rather large, and his influence at the time, and after his death, was so widespread that people took his word on practically every subject.

From the third century BCE, until the 15th century CE, scientists believed a number of things Aristotle thought up. When scientists observed the natural world with better tools and found that Aristotle's geocentric model was incorrect, others followed suit. Slowly, his works on biology were found to be incorrect by William Harvey. The heliocentric model was hardly a new idea when it was proved to be true in the 1800s with Halley's Comet. The first inklings of this idea went as far back as 300BC, but Aristotle's word was considered to be so true that questioning his works was an unthinkable act, perhaps even heresy, by some standards.

We know today that Aristotle was wrong on a number of accounts—his geocentric model of the universe, his view that some men were born to be slaves and that women are somehow incomplete versions of men, among other things—and it has become popular to bash him for it. Some accounts go so far as to say that Aristotle was the reason for the detour in our 2000-year scientific progress.

Democritus, a Greek philosopher born before Aristotle, believed that atoms *must* exist. His mind experiment was simply this: If we keep splitting something, we must get a point where we can't split it anymore. This indivisible "object" is what he considered to be the atom. He was partially right in his atomic theory, in that the world is made up of atoms, but wrong in that we can't split them any further: we now know they can be further split into electrons, protons, and neutrons.

This theory was rejected by Aristotle, who thought that all materials on earth were made of the small amounts of the four classical elements: Fire, Air, Water, and Earth. For more than two thousand years, this knowledge, along with other misconceptions of how the universe operated, misguided our attempts at understanding our own human predicament.

The history of our belief in Aristotle's works and our subsequent change of heart is a very clear example of the downsides of believing one man, or one philosophy, or one written work, so rigidly. The Christian church and the scientists found that much of what they took for granted with Aristotle's work was wrong with regards to our cosmology, which led to further questioning and a better understanding of the universe we inhabit.

To read religious literature for spiritual progress can be beneficial, but to use it to make absolute claims about our reality, to predict our future, to enslave and bully fellow human beings, to destroy the beauty of the only experience of life we have, is another.

Books are time machines, and capsules of memories left to us by those who wanted to share a thought, a finding, a discovery about how the world works, and how we can survive and thrive in it. In that sense, they are almost magical in their ability to let us talk to someone a few millennia away. But to take their word, any word, without questioning says very little about the writer and more about he who reads it. Perhaps authors of religious literature left us a guide to survive in the world as they saw it, and not the world that we experience today. The invention of the internet, of telecommunications, of flight, the discovery of stars far beyond our own sun, are among things they couldn't possibly imagine.

When we read a book or hear a thought, we first question its validity and relevance to our world. If it's invalid or irrelevant, we ignore or refute it. If we read a book on how to use floppy disks a hundred years from now, or even today, we wouldn't possibly all start using floppies just because there is a book that suggests how to use them and references them as a revolution in storage technology. This metaphor is a long stretch, but it makes the point. Yes, the writer is responsible for his writing, but it's not necessary that the writing stays true throughout the course of human evolution.

*

Islam *itself* is not to blame. Rumi, the creator of some of the most beautiful verses known to man was a follower of Islam, he preached love, and his works inspire courage and beauty even today. Rumi's writings speak of oneness with the divine, though they do not conclusively define that divinity. Sometimes his poetry speaks of longing for *the one*, but this "one" may variously be considered to be *god,* a lover, or another human being[45]. Rumi lived and created his legacy in what we now call the Islamic Golden Age.

His work is but one of the many cultural influences found in this era. For five centuries in the Islamic world (from 8th to 13th century CE), there was a heavy patronization of scholars, increased focus on the value of acquiring knowledge, creation of global intellectual centers like the House of Wisdom, and countless inventions that still are a major part of human life today.

The Quranic teachings and the Hadith[46] both valued the acquisition of knowledge, and to that end, Caliphs during the era heavily patronized scholars from different cultural backgrounds to acquire and translate all of the world's knowledge into Arabic. This inevitably helped grow the sciences, economies, and the Islamic culture. The House of Wisdom was but one finale in our quest for acquiring and organizing knowledge.

As the Alexandrian library was the result of the copying of all transcripts that arrived at the ports in Alexandria, and saving the originals in the library; so the House of Wisdom was the translation of scientific and literary works brought about by scholars of different background and beliefs.

But far from being only an academic and scholarly center of learning, these scholars doubled as engineers, architects, doctors, and public servants and made significant contributions to mathematics, astronomy, and physics among other disciplines. It was at this time that the first astronomical observatory was financed.

The House of Wisdom was also created by a *caliphate*. This center of learning and thought, though, was really a gradual development rather than the precursor of the Islamic golden age. Various learning centers developed over the three centuries preceding the House of Wisdom, aimed at developing the sciences and acquiring knowledge there was to be acquired. The House of Wisdom was modeled after the Academy of Gundishapur, one of three intellectual centers of a Persian Empire that existed before the rise of Islamic empires.

In the reading of the past and our history, events such as the founding of the House of Wisdom help act as convenient points of reference of the different eras in our shared history. The blanket terms such as "The Dark Ages", "The Golden Age of the Gupta Empire", "The Renaissance Period", and "The Golden Age of Islam" are some names given to time periods retrospectively. It makes for easier communication among us, and a collective understanding of a time period; as we've seen with the term "dark ages", these terms can also sometimes be misleading.

In reality, all of our discoveries, inventions, and acquisition of knowledge are catalysts for future gradual developments, but they build on our inventions and discoveries of the past. We, in turn, update our knowledge as new discoveries are made for the future generations to come.

Take paper, for instance. It is said that two Chinese prisoners showed the Muslims how the Chinese developed paper. The people of the Islamic world, seeing how practical it would be to write on something that couldn't be erased, like papyrus, took those secrets and developed it into something that could be mass produced, creating a whole industry around it. For the first time in human history, and almost 4000 years since writing was first developed, people could make a living just by writing and selling books. First developed in 100 BCE, it took around 900 years for paper to become ubiquitous:

> *"Paper, originally, was brought by the Muslims from China. It followed the battle of Tallas (751) fought between Chinese and Muslims, when Chinese prisoners revealed the secret of papermaking to the Muslims. From an art, the Muslims developed it into a major industry. The Muslims employed linen as a substitute for the bark of the mulberry, which the Chinese used. Linen rags were disintegrated, saturated with water, and made to ferment. The boiled rags were then cleared of alkaline residue and much of the dirt, and then the rags were beaten to a pulp by the use of a trip hammer, an improved method of maceration invented by the Muslims."[47]*

Each portion of our society has learned from another and contributed something that can leave us inspired if we only try to look for it. Each segment has also learned from another and developed on that knowledge to bring us to where we are today: not just looking at the stars, but making plans to reach them.

In thinking about what we leave for our progeny, it is

easy to forget what has been passed onto us from our predecessors. The anecdotes in this book perhaps touch on a fraction of what is both beautiful and horrific about our past. But what we see is a clear human need for progress, for the stability of our communities, for the victory of our knowledge and understanding of our world. If we don't look back and understand the value of the beautifully interconnected treasure that has been given to us to safeguard, if we don't comprehend the responsibilities that come with it, how can we each protect and empower those who will come after us, who may answer questions we may not be able to answer today?

Where did our individual responsibilities go? Have we taught and practiced compassion where we can? These were *our* ancestors who gave us so much to live for today—and they might have been products of a different world than ours. They may be products of a different time and a different environment when social norms were different. But they unite us by giving us what we can use today to further ourselves—knowledge and wisdom, the sciences and the arts, inventions, and discoveries that make us wonder if they were truly *so* barbaric in their thinking. Mustn't we pride ourselves in their accomplishments? Mustn't we be humbled that we wouldn't be where we are if it wasn't for what they left us?

As we develop our thinking, build on values and ideas of the past, is it really fair for us to destroy generations of cultural and intellectual development for our temporal beliefs? For that which is lost to time may never be recovered again.

*

The same technologically-*on* world that protects our knowledge as organizations and individuals threaten to destroy them has a downside to it. As we are instantly and constantly fed with everything that we desire online, in the real world, it may seem like things may not really change within our lifetimes. It might seem like the only way to "change the world", especially when considering how modern media portrays how *problematic* our world is, is to create a revolution. But to work within the confines of established social structures—political organizations, nonprofit foundations—to affect change can seem futile in the short term.

To an impatient visionary, the pace of change can seem very slow. We live in a world where disruption is the new norm. Social media drives awareness and affects some changes, and then perhaps forgets about them as fast as it affects the changes. But at least we *do have* a platform to make changes that we believe we should. As we look for meaning in our lives, understanding where we have come from—our common human history—may be a great place to start.

Knowledge and education from the information we now have will not cease until we press pause on our evolution ourselves. Such political and religious issues as these show just how small our thinking can sometimes be. We live in a world where on the one hand, we create marvelous new things, and on the other, we find ways to destroy our immediate surroundings. In thinking about our cosmos, our history and the path that lies ahead of us, there is no way in which we can justify actions of such unnecessary destruction fairly. Regional wars and destruction aside, with so much at stake, it is unlikely that we are *naive enough* to launch nuclear missiles to put an end to our own growth and the exploration of our home, but one can never be too sure.

This kind of a communal progress only works if everyone has the same standards of morality, of values and of oneness. It works only if everyone is willing to adhere to the same rules of the game, respecting each other's beliefs and finding common ground with which to move forward. But to believe that all human beings will adhere to the same kind of thinking may seem immature, even naïve. The answer to this is nothing but that we keep trying, over and over again, until we all understand how to behave as *one*.

*

Carl Sagan, in 1994, wrote the following piece about how our nationalist or fundamentalist views matter so little in the grand scheme of things stays relevant to us today. It is worth reading and re-reading because we tend to forget that we are products, creations, students, and children of this world. We don't know what our ultimate purpose is, but we know that we can understand the universe in which we live, one little bit at a time.

"Look again at that dot. That's here. That's home. That's us. On it everyone you love, everyone you know, everyone you ever heard of, every human being who ever was, lived out their lives. The aggregate of our joy and suffering, thousands of confident religions, ideologies, and economic doctrines, every hunter and forager, every hero and coward, every creator and destroyer of civilization, every king and peasant, every young couple in love, every mother and father, hopeful child, inventor and explorer, every teacher of morals, every corrupt politician, every "superstar," every "supreme leader," every saint and sinner in the history of our species lived there--on a mote of dust suspended in a sunbeam.

The Earth is a very small stage in a vast cosmic arena. Think of the rivers of blood spilled by all those generals and emperors so that, in glory and triumph, they could become the momentary masters of a fraction of a dot. Think of the endless cruelties visited by the inhabitants of one corner of this pixel on the scarcely distinguishable inhabitants of some other corner, how frequent their misunderstandings, how eager they are to kill one another, how fervent their hatreds.

Our posturings, our imagined self-importance, the delusion that we have some privileged position in the Universe, are challenged by this point of pale light. Our planet is a lonely speck in the great enveloping cosmic dark. In our obscurity, in all this vastness, there is no hint that help will come from elsewhere to save us from ourselves.

The Earth is the only world known so far to harbor life. There is nowhere else, at least in the near future, to which our species could migrate. Visit, yes. Settle, not yet. Like it or not, for the moment the Earth is where we make our stand.

It has been said that astronomy is a humbling and character-building experience. There is perhaps no better demonstration of the folly of human conceits than this distant image of our tiny world. To me, it underscores our responsibility to deal more kindly with one another, and to preserve and cherish the pale blue dot, the only home we've ever known."

- Carl Sagan, Pale Blue Dot, 1994

Taking pride in our history, in our nations, and in our religious beliefs can be a great thing. It can instill us with confidence, with a sense of belonging and with a sense of security, but doing so at the risk of losing all objectivity of our own communal development can be a very problematic thing: for our individual selves, for our communities, and for our species. ∞

Chapter 8

The Ways in Which We Lie

"There is no absolute knowledge. And those who claim it, whether they are scientists or dogmatists, open the door to tragedy. All information is imperfect. We have to treat it with humility. That is the human condition..."—Jacob Bronowski

Over the six-thousand-year span of our recorded knowledge, we've created and executed some fantastic stuff. Looking back at some of those philosophies, pieces of art, discoveries and technologies—we cannot but be proud of how far we've come. But, in the passing and adopting of this knowledge and wisdom, sometimes we've developed on them in ways that were detrimental to our survival as a species.

The ideas of absolute truth and "the only way to live" still dominate the minds of men. What started as philosophic musings about the nature and cause of our world sometimes became dogmatic, unchanging belief. Religions, nationalistic tendencies, and many organizations exist on the basis of belief of what is "right" and what is "wrong". At one point, the text of the Bible, the Quran, the Gita and the Vedas, the Buddhist Pali texts were not canonized. They were being discovered, written, rewritten, understood, and questioned. When these texts became Canon—that is, found their ultimate form— we, as the recipients of these texts, only saw the final form. We accepted that this is how these texts must always have been. In fact, as we have seen, many of these religions and ideas developed over time, rather than coming into existence in their final form as we see them today. Men and women like us asked the questions that developed these texts. If we look back at our intellectual evolution, we can safely say that many different religions, many different ways of life led to what we collectively call success.

If there is *one* right way to live, we don't know it yet. Over our six thousand years of recorded history, we've built ideas upon ideas and course corrected as we went along. The process of evolution itself is a trial and error mechanism and develops life in a similar way as we develop our intellectual prowess. While evolution is in no rush, the speed of our intellectual evolution is exponential, and we *are in a rush,* possibly because our time on this earth is short. The only cure to some of these intellectual misgivings is knowledge, wisdom, and compassion, and perhaps, time.

Many times, we can't change the points of view of

other people. We can only change our own behavior, our responses, and ultimately hope that we evolve in our understanding of our world. So it is important that we must start with an understanding of the intellectual and psychological pitfalls that we are prone to, as only partially perfect beings of this world.

Being biased towards what we already believe to be true, and how we accept and disseminate information are two sides of the same coin: Confirmation bias and Framing.

Confirmation Bias

Confirmation bias may occur in all human beings in different subjects. Persons of science—those who prefer to observe and interpret—are not immune to this tendency either. If those of us who base a majority of our decisions on observable and provable facts fall prey to mental errors, who's to say that the rest of us don't succumb to the same irrational mental model? Being a man of science doesn't necessarily mean that one is faultless or a superior human being—we are all human, equally capable and equally worthy of creation, but the pursuit of science is the pursuit of probable theories which are true in a set of circumstances.

Confirmation bias makes logical sense: we would selectively be biased towards ideas, facts, and concepts that agree with our worldview. But it is problematic because we tend to agree with things we already believe to be true; i.e., we are biased towards those things we believe in. In studies where subjects were presented with facts that disprove something they believe in, they are skeptical towards those facts. If that information stands corrected, subjects easily accept the error of the first set of facts, effectively *confirming* their *bias* towards what they agree with in the first place. Similarly, if the order was reversed, participants would choose the second set of facts rather than the first because they already believe the second set of facts to be true.

This can be a real problem. How are we to ever accept things as they are if we don't question our beliefs outright? How can we know that something we believe in may be incorrect? And why do we fall prey to ways of thinking that can be so primitive? Our thinking may be motivated by different reasons: our unwillingness to be wrong, our desire for a positive self-image, or our fear of losing a fundamental aspect of our reality, among other things.

When presented with certain facts, if those facts don't agree with our beliefs, we are skeptical because it's hard for us to believe we are wrong. After all, *how can I be wrong?* Many confirmation biases are self-serving and may be motivated by a desire for a positive self-image. Statements that appeal to our unwillingness to be wrong are easily accepted. So are statements of facts that appeal to our willingness to accept something because it makes us feel good about who we are. By extension, we are less agreeable to statements that generate doubt or discomfort in us.

The types of biases we tend to have are very telling.

We can be biased towards or against specific groups of people (Americans are so and so, or the Brits are so and so), or certain consistent actions of people (He's always late, or She's always charming), or the likelihood of something happening ("terrorists" are also followers of Islam).

Confirmation bias can also be based on the desirability of the outcome: for instance, believers in Christianity are more likely to believe in the second coming of Jesus than non-believers, or alternatively, non-believers are *very* unlikely to believe that Jesus would be resurrected.

In deciding what information to accept, our minds take shortcuts based on our accepted beliefs. This is obviously helpful in situations where we are in a time crunch and need to make decisions quickly, but these biases can be dangerous to our personal and intellectual growth. We may never learn new information or world views if we only accept what we've always accepted.

Framing

The other side of this coin is how stories are written, told, and shared. While confirmation bias depends on the consumer of certain information, *framing* depends on the creator or originator of this information. Humans have a general tendency to accept only the information that helps our cause or believe in something when it is framed in ways that agree with our points of view, even if the underlying facts remain the same.

Any given fact can be stated in many different ways, depending on the version of the story one wishes to enforce. We love stories that we can relate to. The way we frame an event, the suspense or feeling it creates and the context a story gives us about the world in which we live, can be incredibly meaningful. But stories can be framed in different ways without changing the underlying facts. The famous exercise of emphasizing on each of the words in "*I never said she stole my money*" is very telling of how we say something changes what we say.

Try it for yourself.

- **I** *never said she stole my money,* implying someone else did
- *I never said* **she** *stole my money,* implying someone did steal, but it wasn't *her*
- *I never said she stole* **my** *money,* implying she did steal someone's money

The emphasis on any one word in this statement implies *she* stole money and effectively discards the speaker's responsibility in the information conveyed. Whether she stole the money or not is unclear and isn't representative of any of the underlying facts. While this is a fun exercise used in leadership and professional courses, this exercise illuminates the underlying nature of the way human beings communicate.

In writing and in life, we deeply *frame* our arguments.

Our viewpoints, and even objective truths, define the lens through which we view the world and how we enable others to view the world through our lens. The act of *framing* is to put a lens on certain events and give the stories context, as they appear to happen in the natural or the social world[48]. Framing a story or a fact is to share a point of view. These frames can be based on natural events or the social factors that drive them. While Natural framing looks at events as they occur in the natural world, social framing looks at the influence of the players in the event.

A fairly basic example of a natural frame is a statement such as "Whales die in South Pacific". This event has occurred in the natural world—a whale has died in the South Pacific—and we, as readers or receivers of this information, have no context of the natural or social factors that caused it. Social framing, on the other hand, builds on the natural framework to describe, interpret or imply intelligent control. The same natural frame above can be turned into a social framework like this: "Whales die in South Pacific, Oil Executives Questioned". This frame adds a layer of social element to the natural framework, and yet, the outcome is quite different.

The statement above doesn't tell us whether the oil industry executives were involved in any way, but it leads us to believe that they had a part to play in the death of whales. Perhaps they were, perhaps not. The reader is induced to fill in the missing information—as our brains are so adept at doing: maybe a shipment of oil broke and spilled into the ocean, effectively killing a whale. This kind of framing can be done consciously or unconsciously.

The example above is one example of different forms framing takes. Of course, not all frames are negative, and not all frames induce readers to fill in information that is incorrect. Some frames make our views more diverse and increase our understanding of the world in which we live. Reading both fiction and non-fiction books, watching movies or documentaries, reading articles on the web are some ways in which we agree to let someone else frame a story and share with us. It is with framing that we can improve the way we view the world by understanding diverse perspectives. We not only understand a different interpretation of the facts but also understand why they are interpreted differently.

It is through framing that we understand that events in the natural or social world have both those who support and those who oppose those events. There are those who benefit from any given event and those who lose something due to it. Very few events can be considered absolutely positive for all the parties involved, if any. ∞

Chapter 9

Are We Ready?

"Science and technology revolutionize our lives, but memory, tradition and myth frame our response."—Arthur M. Schlesinger

Framing is an innate part of the human experience. We frame every experience that we share depending on where we stand with regards to an issue. Myths and legends that are passed to us through the generations are generally constructed within the frame of a *hero who saves the world, conquers evil, and defeats the villain who's out to destroy something good.*

References to Asian or African developing countries conjures up images of these countries being primitive or undeveloped in their entirety. This is a result of years of framing stories in ways that implied, interpreted, or inferred facts to suggest that entire countries lack modern development.

Stories about life in Hollywood conjure up margaritas by the pool, bikini-clad women, and men with six pack abs and a tan. Music videos, tabloid magazines, and reality TV shows have incorporated these as basic features of anyone living a Hollywood life. That is their frame, but the reality may be quite different.

One reason for such framing is because news media is focused on events that address our hopes and fears—terrorist attacks, local crime, shootouts or political issues engage the fear of viewers. Pool parties and sunny days spent by the pool engage us with our hopes for such a life for ourselves. Perhaps we live vicariously through those in the music videos or reality shows.

Attitudes towards issues, and by extension our frame of those issues, are not just about two or more sides to an issue. It has to do with the way our world operates: Every event that occurs in the world has multiple effects, and some of those effects are positive, and others aren't.

Our attitudes and beliefs not only change depending on our knowledge, but they change over time as well. Tom and Jerry, the internationally famous children's cartoon television program, is an excellent, if simplistic, example of attitudes changing over time. Children prefer to associate with Jerry— the fun loving rascal of a mouse who's always up to some mischief—making life interesting.

Then there's Tom, whom children love to hate. Some

children may use Tom as an insult to their peers or adults, implying that they suck the fun out of everything or limit the extent of their activities. As a grown up, our views on this change drastically. Tom seems to be more relatable once we get older. He's only just trying to save the cheese from being eaten by a mouse. He's only just trying to stay out of trouble or keep the house in good order. Our experiences change our views and our attitudes.

It is naïve to think that we will never change our views on certain subjects—it may even be dangerous to believe so. As we go through life, our experiences change the way we perceive things and people around us.

Framing isn't just a tool for writers to inspire messages or for media agencies to set an agenda. Understanding what framing is and how it affects the messages we receive is important to readers as well. It is a tool to aid in thinking, to discern fact from opinion, and to understand that facts take many different forms, depending on the vantage point from which one looks at it.

It is one of many techniques that aids in critical thinking and the understanding of an idea or issue holistically. Without this understanding, we are prone to gullibility or accepting misinformation about issues that affect us as individuals, societies, and species.

*

While "truth" *may be* subjective, the continuity of our species depends on some critical factors. Food, oxygen, and water being among them. We ought to have an understanding that although some interpretations of facts about things happening in the natural world may take different forms, the effects are ours to bear, no matter how we frame the underlying facts.

One impending disaster threatening life on earth that gets less than its share of screen time is the amount of trees we are losing day after day. The gravity of this loss is virtually impossible to overstate. Without a substantial amount of trees covering the earth, living on our planet would be nearly impossible. Some of the recent statistics, or "facts", regarding the forested land on our earth follow[49]:

- Forests cover about 31% of our land as of 2010.
- We deforested and logged about 13-16 million hectares (.03% of forests) per year.
- On average, the forest area grew by about 7-8 million hectares (50% of the forest cut) yearly in some areas.

Deforestation is a short-term and a long-term problem for humanity. Plants and trees, and by extension forests, convert carbon dioxide (what we breathe out) to oxygen (what we breathe in). Increased carbon dioxide in the air leads to an increase in the greenhouse effect, which leads to global warming. Deforestation is one of the direct causes of global warming.

The greenhouse effect is not inherently bad. It is the name given to the effect that keeps our planet warm enough to harbor life. If the heat that was radiated by the sun wasn't trapped in our atmosphere, the average temperature on our planet would be 30 degrees Celsius cooler, or about -15 degrees Celsius (54 degrees Fahrenheit, -5 degrees Fahrenheit respectively). The term greenhouse effect is used negatively in the global warming context, and because of decades of framing, it is generally associated with a negative impact on our environment. Industrialization led to the acceleration of the amount of carbon emitted into the atmosphere, increasing this greenhouse effect.

All human activities release carbon dioxide into the atmosphere. Flying planes, burning coal, powering our appliances through electricity, any process that converts energy emits carbon, and we call this our collective carbon footprint. Just by existing, we breathe out about 2.3 pounds of carbon dioxide per day, negligibly heating our planet. But the result of the sum of all human activities is not negligible— since industrialization, we have emitted enough carbon *and* burned enough of our forests to increase the average surface temperature of our earth by 1 degree Celsius (1.8 degrees Fahrenheit).

Forests provide biodiversity and may well play a part in the process of evolution over millennia. Most of the deforestation occurs due to our need for agricultural land for growing food, and for logging operations for wood and paper products. Other reasons for deforestation include urbanization of land and natural causes like wildfires. In the course of the past few decades, many countries have lost massive forested lands due to legal and illegal logging operations. So, how can we prevent our world from disintegrating due to a lack of forested land?

We could plant more trees, and we could find ways to not use as many resources as we do, among other things. If we truly understood the effects of our actions, we would be planting *more* trees, and cutting down fewer of them.

As we increase the amount of carbon in our atmosphere, we must be increasing the sources that will deplete that carbon, negating the effects of our activities. But this logic fails here. What matters to us is not the long term effects of our actions, but the pacification of our desires in the short term. If we need food, we find food. If we need shelter, we build shelter.

To see better at night, we invented electricity. To get to places faster, we invented cars, planes, and now spaceships. All human actions have a snowball effect that can be either detrimental or beneficial. It is, of course, impractical to see all different angles before solving a problem—one may never solve it if one doesn't take a stand. It may even be impossible to predict the chain reactions our actions unleash.

In a timeline-oriented and results-driven world, thinking about the long term effects goes counter to our professional development. One may be considered inept if he isn't able to act and deliver. But to know the side effects of our actions and not do anything about it seems to be an invitation to our own demise as a species.

*

Based on the information provided so far, it is clear that deforestation is a threat to our existence in the long term. All of what we have developed and have to live for is at risk of eradication if we don't have a planet we can call home. "Truth" in this scenario may be different based on who we're talking to. Some people believe that global warming is a hoax.

In terms of *framing* this story, the frame with which we look at this story is based on the facts provided: Forests are good for "us", forests are being cut down, and therefore, that's not good. The same story and the same facts can be presented in a different way[50].

Depending on who provides us a frame, the information we get can differ. Organizations destroying swathes of forest land may provide us with a completely different version of these facts. They may focus on how much of our area is being reforested consistently while our deforestation rate has decreased. We may be presented with facts about the jobs and opportunities such deforestation provides. People interested in financial growth may provide governments with different facts that suit their purpose.

Indonesia, a country in South-east Asia has lost about 40% of its forest area in 5 decades. Other developing countries in South America and Sub-Saharan Africa suffer a similar fate. Those making policy decisions are driven to decide policy based on factors other than just these facts. Lobbying and relationships also play a part in how policies relating to climate change and deforestation are enforced.

At each stage, someone may view the same effect of deforestation differently. Officers of the law may not enforce the law for those who cut the trees because it affects their livelihood. Lobbyists are *paid* to influence policy decisions regardless of the effects of those decisions. Some of the logging of these forests is illegal, and trees are cut down with no one to regulate this activity. Each actor on this stage has a responsibility towards what is collectively *agreed* to be good for us—the survival of our species. When presented with facts, we cannot deny those effects that threaten the livelihood of the future of our species.

While we can frame facts in any way we want, the underlying facts that affect us remain the same. It is only by truly caring about our causes—our passion for our world and the continuity of our existence—can we truly take the time out to find out what's really going on in the world out there. It is only by looking at our species as one can we ensure that we take steps towards our own survival. Our religions, nationalist tendencies, and the things we love will matter very little if there is no place for us in which to exist and thrive.

*

The people who burn books are often people who don't read books of varied and diverse viewpoints. We can't change people, and we shouldn't want to—if we are to accept diverse viewpoints and appreciate the uniqueness and individuality in each of us. But we can start today by educating our children and instilling them with a sense of wonder that comes with knowing and accepting the diversity of thought in our age. We can start today by educating ourselves about our shared history and the future we can create together—not just as individuals but collectively as human beings.

Even so, things look up. Availability of information is better than unavailability, even with different viewpoints, different versions of truth. We are able to pick our beliefs based on facts or faith, and course correct as different and new information is uncovered. Our intellectual and cultural growth, as we've seen time and again, is dependent on a diversity of opinions and ideas.

Belief and acceptance in one idea, one philosophy, and a dogmatic belief in a single correct way of life is detrimental to our development and our survival. "Truths" about our world can be different in different places and different time periods. Some of these truths can take different forms. They can be:

> **Individual truths:** What is true about the nature or physiology of an individual? What is right or wrong for *me* to do? What do I believe the world is?
>
> **Societal/Communal truths:** What is accepted to be true by a society or a group of people? What is

considered right or wrong? Ethics and Morality may be devised on a societal level, the existence or non-existence of a God or Gods is an example.

Cosmological truths: The way our world operates. Do we live in a heliocentric universe? Is our universe infinite? What do we accept to be true about our world today but may not have always been the case? While we once believed that we were *created,* we later came to understand that we may have evolved, some scientists posit that we may just be a simulation in another being's computer.

The thing about our reality is that we collectively accept certain things to be true, and as we ask more questions and acquire more answers, what we perceive to be our "reality" changes. Because of the subjectivity of our experience and how we communicate with each other, it is very hard for us to define and experience objective reality directly and easily.

For instance, the discovery of Quarks changed the way we perceive and theorize about matter. Quarks are subatomic particles that make up protons and neutrons, and are the building blocks of matter, along with leptons. Up until the discovery of electrons in 1897 and quarks in 1968, we considered atoms to be the smallest particles in our world[51].

John Dalton, in the early 1800s, theorized about the atoms, and until 1897, we couldn't prove even an atom's existence. It took us only 70 years to divide the smallest particle theorized by man for 2 millennia. In some walks of life, these discoveries uncovered a whole new world which we didn't know existed before. It took us about 2200 years to find evidence of the existence of an atom, and to divide it a few times only took us 70 years.

Our reality changes depending on what we know and understand. The questions we ask define our experience, and these changes in experience need not be our experience collectively as a species. Individual "realities" change the same way. The way one perceives the world changes depending on one's knowledge of the world.

From a religious standpoint, some individuals pick up religions later on in life; some others give it up in favor of atheism or agnosticism. From a human standpoint, many individuals improve their communication skills later on in life, become more loving, giving and nurturing; and yet others become harsher, more aggressive and less tolerant.

These changes depend on the length and depth of our experience. A diffident individual might at first be less assertive than he would like, but upon "having had enough" of life and being subjugated, he grows into someone more aggressive or assertive than his previous self.

It is not unheard of that fundamental beliefs of people change over time. Questioning the things we previously took for granted, and increasing our knowledge about our past and the world we live in can certainly help us become more well-rounded individuals. How we perceive the world, and subsequently our individual reality, changes based on what we experience and the content we consume about the world. Absolute knowledge, then, is a myth. We can only be 99.99% sure of anything.

What we believe to be true can be only based on the facts that we know *so far*, or our faith. We are good at correcting things that don't favor our evolution as a species. Perhaps there will come a day when we are able to correct our biases and be rational thinkers in totality. With each passing generation, we are less superstitious and more scientific than we once were.

Some, if not most, of our past is mired with superstition. The belief in magic, in pseudoscience, in ghosts, in spirits existed in most societies of men and it still exists today. While we cannot prove the existence of ghosts and magic and other pseudoscience, we cannot disprove it. Of course, it is impossible to say confidently that these things do not exist, no matter how improbable they may seem. Just as we saw in the history of the atom, it is possible that we do not yet have the tools to look beyond. But, there is a degree of certainty with which we can address these issues *now*, and conclude that the chances of them existing are very slim given our current knowledge and tools.

About a third of the people surveyed by HuffPost/YouGov believe in ghosts[52]. Of course, this number may be different in different communities and different age groups. But surveys like this bring to light an interesting underlying fact: we are still prone to absolutely believing in things we cannot prove, on gut feeling alone. A statement like "ghosts exist" is not absolutely incorrect, but a better version may be that "we have no way of proving whether or not ghosts exist". One may replace ghosts with anything else, but the point remains.

With no way to answer what the stars were, we postulated that they were perhaps holes in the sky or that they were souls of our dead relatives. Many other cultures came up with more creative, larger narratives around the existence of stars and what they mean:

> *"Chinese mythology includes many references to the stars. Various deities, such as the god of literature and the god of long life, were associated with the stars. One myth that occurs in several versions concerns the Weaver Girl, the goddess who weaves the clouds, and the Herdsman, who tends the cattle of heaven. The two were lovers. When the gods placed them in the sky, the Weaver Girl became the star called Vega, while the Herdsman became either the star Altair or the constellation Aquila. The gods separated the lovers with the river of the Milky Way so that they would not neglect their work. But every year, on the seventh night of the seventh month, birds formed a bridge across the Milky Way*

allowing the Weaver Girl and the Herdsman to meet."—A Chinese myth[53]

Plato wrote that each soul on earth had a companion star, and upon death of the being, the soul went back to the star as long as it had lived a just life. If someone were to tell us these versions of their story today, and perhaps suggest that it was true, we would call him a madman, or at best a man with a creative imagination. We know now that the sun is a star, and that the stars are bright objects in distant galaxies far away from us. But this wasn't "true" a few millennia ago. People couldn't fathom that an infinite cosmos could exist, much less believe it. People couldn't believe that the earth was round, or that the sun was at the center of our solar system— it just didn't make sense when we observed it.

While the subjectivity of truth is ubiquitous, and we are starting to understand this, the underlying facts that lay in front of us require more of our fair and unbiased attention: regardless of how they're framed, how we feel about them or whether or not we like to hear it. ∞

Chapter 10

To Believe or Not To Believe

"After the game, the king and the pawn go back in the same box"—Italian Proverb.

We believe because it gives us faith. It gives us the willingness to go through our day, to keep the existentialist threat of meaninglessness away. We believe because we crave to be seen, to be known, to be understood. We believe because that is the only thing we can do. If there is no one to judge us— to tell us that we are good, and that if we are bad, we can be redeemed—why bother living at all? Why bother being good at all? If there is no one to look after us, and we are truly alone in this universe, what purpose do we have? We have nothing but the present moment, and in the grand scheme of things, only temporariness.

The prospect of that is truly horrific when we consider

how much we value our lives. The very reason for our existence today is our survival instincts embedded in our DNA. We cling to our dear lives because that's what helps us exist, conquer and thrive for eons.

We, of all the beings that we know of, can think. We can eat, write, build, save. We can predict, estimate, and count. We can preserve food for lifetimes, and in times of crisis, we can find ways to ensure our survival. With each passing generation, our sphere of control on our existence is larger. What if the earth is hit by an asteroid or there is no way to stop global warming? We look to colonize other planets. The fate of our species, in a few years, will not be tied to the fate of the earth. Our home planet must be cared for, and nurtured, as it has nurtured us, but as we go interplanetary and then interstellar, our control on our lives and the evolution of our species grows. As far as we know, we are the only species that has a say in the development of its future.

If these statements are true, then it is easy to believe that we are the chosen ones. It is easy to shed humility and adopt arrogance. We conjecture that life is what we make of it, or that the purpose of life is for each individual to live a good and virtuous life, or to find material success. But what are we chosen for? We have no clues as to the meaning or the reason for our existence.

That there is something good waiting for us on the other side of the wall of death is not just a premise of one religion or a belief of one phase of our humanity. We have collectively found creative ways, time and again, to make our life worth more than just this temporary existence.

We theorize that perhaps, if there is a god, he/she/it redeems us and gives us meaning. That if there is no god, then we—and the world around us—could not come to exist. The likelihood of our existence is so miraculously low that we cannot fathom that we may not have been created and that we evolved through a trial and error process over billions of years.

We cannot accept or imagine that we are products of random chance. Everything we see around us exists the way it does because the environment on our planet was just right. Do we not give ourselves more credit than we do to our universe if we believe that we are so special that only a god can create us? It is because of our environment that we came to exhibit our current features. A few differences in the composition of our atmosphere would mean that we would turn out to be completely different beings—or worse, not exist at all. If the dinosaurs didn't go extinct when they did, chances are that the evolution of our ancestors may have been very different.

A few changes in our timeline would mean massive changes in the development of our species. But we *have* come to exist, and only we can build walls, develop machinery, write literature, and compose symphonies. Our pleasures in this world are infinite, and we don't have enough time to experience even a tiny fraction of it.

But what is the purpose of religion? It makes us "good" human beings, it makes us fearful of what might happen if we do not follow the word of the gods. It gives us a fundamental security that cannot be taken away from us because, after all, gods will look after us as long as we adhere to their words.

That fundamental security that religion provides becomes a delusion very quickly. When we interact with people of different faiths, or no faith at all, we come to face the reality of different gods created by different cultures over time. These questions and the resulting interactions can very quickly lead to violence. The same gods that make us fearful and *good*, also tell us that we mustn't submit to another god, and that violence is an acceptable measure in these situations. These are hard contradictions to reconcile. An over simplification of how we learned from each other's religion and developed the history of our religion follows:

A: "My god is a strong god"

B: "My god is even stronger, in fact he is all-knowing and all-powerful"

C: "It makes sense, then, that I should align myself with B's god"

D: "Yeah, why wouldn't you? B's god is stronger than A's god."

This over-simplification is not incorrect, and a reading of our history of religion tells us this. We gradually moved from polytheistic religions to monotheistic religions as we attributed more power to our gods. The first religions, in Mesopotamia, gave the gods rule over the things we could see: we had a god of earth, of the sky, of water, of the moon and so on. Polytheism continued to be a part of later cultures, as we see in the Greek and Pagan traditions of gods being the caretakers of certain features of our world. This view came to be seen as inferior, as more philosophy developed around the nature of the one supreme divine being. A single, unified, divine being, who rules over the entire cosmos, must implicitly be more powerful than *any other god*. These religions, following a monotheistic—Abrahamic—god, then divulged further.

Christianity, once a part of Judaism, came to believe that Christ was the savior of our world, and the human representation of the omniscient, omnipotent god. He was one of the three parts of the inaccessible and almighty god. Judaism and Islam, both also Abrahamic religions, made no such distinctions. For them, any division of god is not possible, though "he" might be called by different names.

This is, of course, a very brief and largely western look at the development of religions. Which one of us is right? Gods don't need defending, if they exist. It is our beliefs in them that need to be defended. It is our security as individuals and communities that is threatened when our beliefs are questioned or overthrown. Our fear of losing our identity, if we associate strongly with the belief in question, kicks in and we are on our way to destruction shortly thereafter.

The fear of something bigger than us keeps us grounded and good individuals. Belief can unite or divide people, and the more people believe in something, the stronger that belief gets. This doesn't make that belief the only possibility, it just means that it makes *sense* to that many people at that given time.

We can only probably say whether the world was created or evolved. We can't even definitely say what caused the world to exist in the first place if we consider that which we can observe. The knowledge of the ages has grown tremendously over the course of the last six thousand years of our recorded history. We know more now than we did before, and we will continue to build on that knowledge. As we observe more, build more intricate tools to look further into space or deeper into atoms, we will be certain about more things than we are now.

The why of our creation may never be answered in our lifetimes, but that doesn't stop us from speculating. It is a marvel that we have so many different theories not just about how the world came to be but also about what the world *is*. Aren't these theories worth a look? Wouldn't we want to know, on the basis of facts, what our home could be in the broadest sense? What we see when we look around is perhaps a few kilometers, a couple of miles. Looking around every minute, we can see only so little, and our minds are pre-programmed to work only on that scale. Some of us manage to think bigger, brighter, deeper thoughts. Some of these thoughts already shape the kind of research we do. Some of them will prove to be right, and our understanding of our home will deepen. Our home, one day, will be less of a mystery to us. ∞

Chapter 11

Those Who Forget History

"The best way to predict your future is to create it"—
Abraham Lincoln

The forgetfulness of the past may be what makes human life so hopeful in the first place. This ability to pick up pieces, move on in the face of adversity is incredibly human and incredibly amazing. As a species, we have the grit and the perseverance to solve unimaginably complex problems—and we do not back down. The questions we can't answer keep coming back to us. The things we don't know now *will* be answered in the lifetimes to come. That which we know now was unknown to most humans that ever lived, and this cycle will continue. Our progeny will have answers to questions which we do not.

The Chinese, Greeks, Romans, Indians, Mayans, Incans, all found answers to some of our most fundamental questions, sometimes differently, sometimes in remarkably similar ways. All of our cultures found ways to share and preserve each other's books, thoughts, and ideas, to learn from other cultures and to utilize and improve each other's inventions. This world we live in today, all of our knowledge is now shared with each other on an unimaginable scale, available on platforms accessible to a majority of us. Books are being digitized, information is being transformed and is available to us in any form we wish to consume it in— audiobooks, videos, movies, documentaries, e-books, and of course, in physical form.

While the six thousand years leading up to this moment have been mired with the loss of information, the *problem* we face today is that of too much: too much information, too many things to do, and too many sources that give us differing versions of stories. In this world of too much, our main concern is not that we may not know enough, but that we may not be curious enough to ask the right questions or be diligent enough to seek after holistic answers. While not having enough (of anything) pushes us to our limits to seek answers, too much may paralyze our ability to do anything with all of what we have.

If we all don't feel individually responsible for this diligence, we may be doomed to live in a world where we are lost in a myriad of re-spun articles that tell us the *same thing* over and over again. We may be doomed to drown in the information that brought us to this moment in our shared history. Our hope is that until we find a solution for the problem of too much, we take responsibility for the information we consume and create, and question the implication of what we create.

We ought to, as human beings, have the courage to seek a collective "truth" that benefits our species the most, and to accept that all of our doctrines and beliefs *may just* be incomplete. That we don't know it all and that perhaps we never will. That others like us may have something to teach us, and we may have something to contribute to their communities. That communities, *types of people,* are divisions we've created for ourselves. That for all of what we know, the knowledge and wisdom that we have gathered in the few millennia may be a small fraction of what is there to be discovered, understood and applied.

Hindsight is 20-20. Looking back, it is easier for us to reason, and sometimes even give meaning to things that have happened. We create because we must. Our inner drive to make a difference for ourselves, our families, our communities, our nations, and our species makes us look to the future. What are the possibilities that lie in our future?

A thousand years ago, we had no scientific instruments that could look out into space and past into time. Telescopes came around 1600s[54], and until then, all we had about the nature of our cosmos were theories based on what we could see with the naked eye. Some of those theories were more probable than others, some were more intuitive than others. We see ourselves as more powerful, intelligent and bigger than some other species around us, so it was easier to accept that bigger, more powerful, more intelligent beings created us than it was to accept that we may have come to exist because of random chance. We may find that some of what we take for granted is refuted in our future, just as we refute the theories put forward by our ancestors.

Looking into space is really looking back into time. Light travels at about 300 thousand meters per second; sunlight takes a little more than 8 minutes to reach us at a distance of 150 thousand kilometers. So when we're looking at sunlight from the earth, we're really looking at the sun as it was 8 minutes ago. As we see further into space, we also see further back into time. We now have these instruments that can look back into time to almost 14 billion years ago, which is roughly how old our universe is.

Some religious scriptures claim that we are living in a universe that is six millennia old, other religions put that estimate at 300 trillion years old. Human beings, across cultures, time and space, have theorized that our universe is somewhere between six-thousand years to 300 trillion years old, and everything in between.

We may find that something we believed in a few thousand years ago may actually turn out to be true. What we can say today, though, is that we don't really know. All we have is our tools, and our cognition and the overlap of these two tells us how probable or improbable some of our beliefs and ideas are.

Our best bet at knowing if there is indeed an omniscient, omnipresent of even a multitude of semi-scient, semi-omni-present beings, is for that being to present itself in our midst. The rest of the miracles are anecdotal; conjectures based on our need to be cared for, to be loved and accepted, to believe that there is good and evil *outside* of humanity. If there is an omniscient "being", then we don't know *it* and perhaps we never will, but if and as our legacy continues, then we may have a slight chance of *creating* an omniscient or a semi-scient being: a supercomputer that is an aid to the human thirst for knowledge and understanding, able to process all information simultaneously and give us answers to things that we may not be able to connect and interpret. In these connections and interpretations by a cognition larger than us, we may find answers for some of our deepest, most personal questions.

But until then, the least we can do is accept our beliefs for what they are, and look for what is objectively provable. Objective truth has universal applicability—and the wonders of this knowledge are infinitely empowering. To know how the universe operates is a first step in building the world as we want it to be. To be truly honorable to the talent that this universe has bestowed upon us, we must use that talent to ask questions, find ways to answer them and accept the answers, no matter how strange they may seem.

In these cases, *how one feels* or *what one thinks* about

the subject is irrelevant. This may seem unduly irreverent of the feelings of human beings, because after all, our emotions may be what make us human. But if we are to proceed on the course of knowledge—of understanding the world and the universe that we inhabit—we must be accepting of truth as things are rather than how we would like things to be.

To view the Milky Way in the night sky is one of the most beautiful, awe-inducing experiences. Many of us go without seeing the colorful, illustrious wonder that *just kind of exists*. It doesn't matter whether or not someone looks at it[55]. If one has the opportunity to go atop hills or mountains, or areas where the city lights don't crowd out light that comes into our planet from the universe outside, it is a sight to behold. It is a perspective-inducing experience that all human beings ought to experience at least once.

Never before in our shared history have we been able to not only view these wonders, but answer what they may be, and make plans to reach them. Through our communal knowledge, we have built our treasure chest to a point where we are able to answer questions with a certain amount of confidence *and* be honest about what we cannot know.

Our science—one part of our objective worldview—gives us a baseline of how things are. We, communally as human beings, must decide how things *should be*. If deforestation is a threat to our world, if global warming makes our lives unsustainable, if our scriptures and religions make us destructive, *only we* can prevent ourselves from losing perspective of the beauty of this universe and the value of the human life. One only need to look at the depth of our history, the grit of *our people*, and the beauty of the nature of our universe to ensure we leave it in a better state than what we were given. ∞

Thank you for reading this book. If you enjoyed it, please share your experience on amazon.com, goodreads, or your preferred bookshop.

If you did not enjoy this book or had a problem with it, please contact the author at tarun@tarunbetala.com

Appendix & Endnotes

A Very Personal Request

Thank you for reading the book. I am very grateful for your support, and I hope that you enjoyed the process of reading and discovering (or re-discovering) the concepts entailed. Books are supposed to illuminate, entertain, make us question, give answers, and befriend us, among other things. I hope that this book has done that for you.

If you would like to further this discussion, provide feedback, or share your thoughts about the concepts and ideas discussed here, I'm always available on email at tarun@tarunbetala.com and twitter at @trbetala. My website, tarunbetala.com, contains further reading material and a reading guide to this book, which you can download and share for free.

Best,
Tarun

The Epic of Gilgamesh: A Short Summary

The very first epic written by humans, around 3rd Millennium BCE

The epic starts with an introduction to Gilgamesh, a beautiful and strong god-like king of Uruk, who builds temples and surrounds his city with high walls with slaves. Gilgamesh rapes any woman he fancies and oppresses his subjects, who, exhausted, pray to the gods to be saved. The gods heed the pleas of those who are oppressed by Gilgamesh and create a wild man—Enkidu—who is as strong and impressive as Gilgamesh. Enkidu lives in the wild with animals, and to bring him into the civilized human world, a temple harlot is sent. After a sexual initiation, Enkidu is effectively civilized, and the woman then explains Gilgamesh's despotic rule in Uruk to Enkidu.

Enkidu then challenges Gilgamesh as he is on his way to rape another woman, and their fierce fight lasts for a long time with Gilgamesh emerging as the winner. This fight ends in Gilgamesh and Enkidu becoming friends and go looking for adventure together. After an adventure that strengthens their friendship, the goddess of love, Ishtar is overcome with lust for Gilgamesh, who rejects her advances. Furious, Ishtar asks her father, the god of the sky, to send the Bull of Heaven to punish him. Gilgamesh and Enkidu together fight the bull and kill it. This enrages the gods and they meet in council, deciding to kill one of the two friends: Enkidu. The death of his friend affects Gilgamesh deeply, who is overcome with grief over his loss and reflects on his own mortality, the impending event of his own death.

This is a turning point in the life of Gilgamesh, who renounces his kingly robes and wealth, and goes into the forest to find a man who was granted immortality by the gods for having saved humanity from a great flood that threatened to destroy all humankind. In their conversations, Gilgamesh is told that he belongs in Uruk and he should return there and that his search for immortality is futile. After this harrowing search for the immortal, and venturing in faraway lands, Gilgamesh finally realizes that he must go back and live his life as the ruler of Uruk. In a final twist of fate, he is given a plant that restores youth, but one night on his way back to Uruk while camping, a snake steals the plant and the key to youth is lost. As Gilgamesh returns home, he realizes that what he has built—his legacy, the amazing city he created—is one way for him to be immortal and remembered by the humankind that will go on living eons after he is no more. ∞

Further Reading

A free reading guide is available on my website, at tarunbetala.com/reading-guide. You can download, share, and use that as a resource to question the concepts and ideas presented in this book, in your personal reading or your book clubs.

A good place to start for further reading follows, in no particular order:

- *Cosmos*, Carl Sagan
- *Pale Blue Dot*, Carl Sagan
- *The Big Picture*, Sean Carroll
- *God's Philosophers*, John Hannam
- *The Last Question*, Isaac Asimov (Short Story)
- *Brave New World*, Aldous Huxley
- *Gilgamesh: A New English Version,* Stephen Mitchell
- *Meditations*, Marcus Aurelius
- *The Essential Rumi,* translated by Coleman Barks
- *A Brief History of Time*, Stephen Hawking

Where can I see the Milky Way? (http://bzfd.it/2ePIwrb)

Endnotes

[1] Benjamin franklin, was the first to discover that electricity had both positive and negative charges.

[2] A very introductory lesson is available on the NEH website online, along with suggestions for further reading. The Cuneiform Writing System in Ancient Mesopotamia: Emergence and Evolution (http://bit.ly/ttwdk2)

[3] By John Hill, CC BY-SA 3.0 (http://bit.ly/ttwdkf4)

[4] Andrew George and Al-Rawi helped translate the text; Quote from LiveScience, which liaised with George (http://bit.ly/ttwdkf3)

[5] The first attempt at deciphering the script started in 1625 by a Roman traveler to Persepolis, and the decipherment was considered relatively complete in 1857. (http://bit.ly/ttwdkf5-2)

[6] *Pots and Alphabets: Refractions of Reflections on Typological Method* (MAARAV, A Journal for the Study of the Northwest Semitic Languages and Literatures, Vol. 10, p. 89)

7 All Ideas Are Second-Hand: Mark Twain's Magnificent Letter to Helen Keller About the Myth of Originality (http://bit.ly/ttwdkf5)

8 Records do exist of writings being destroyed prior to this. As mentioned in the Hebrew Bible, King Jehoiakim burned a part of the scroll dictated by Jeremiah. *"Also tell Jehoiakim king of Judah, 'This is what the LORD says: You burned that scroll and said, "Why did you write on it that the king of Babylon would certainly come and destroy this land and wipe from it both man and beast?"*

9 In the Chinese classical period (6th–3rd century BCE), the chief concepts were Dao ("the Way"), de ("virtue"), ren ("humanity," "love"), yi ("righteousness"), tian ("heaven"), and yinyang (cosmic elements of tranquility and activity, or weakness and strength, respectively). Every school had its own Way, but the Way of Confucius (551–479 BCE) and that of another traditional sage, Laozi (6th century BCE), were the most prominent. (Britannica, Chinese Philosophy)

[10] Denis Twitchett and John K. Fairbank, 2008. P.74-75 Cambridge History of China.

[11] Later claims that these were Confucian texts. Whether or not these were Confucian texts—writings of the school of Confucianism—are debated. The Han dynasty, which followed Qin, adopted Confucianism as the state religion, along with legalism, so to speak. Shiji, or *The Records of the Grand Historian,* were written during the Han Dynasty.

[12] Yuan, Zhongyi. *China's terracotta army and the First Emperor's mausoleum: the art and culture of Qin Shihuang's underground palace.* Paramus, New Jersey: Homa & Sekey Books, 2010. ISBN 978-1-931907-68-2 (p.140)

[13] Filial Piety, very broadly, is to have respect for one's parents, ancestors and elders.

[14] A 20-page essay on the high-equilibrium trap, an intense and interesting read on why perfection may just be a bad thing. (http://bit.ly/ttwdk-helt)

[15] The earliest records of the use of mercenary armies date as far back as ancient Egypt in the 13th century BCE. Mercenary

Armies still exist today, with private military companies acting on behalf of governments and civil organizations.

16 Moya Mason's article on ancient Alexandria and the life during the time is fascinating and comprehensive enough for a basic understanding of the time. (http://bit.ly/ttwdkf1o)

17 Called Pinakes, Callimachus created this sometime in the 3rd century BCE. The term "pinax" later may have taken on the meaning of catalog, outside the domain of the Alexandrian Library. The model was used for almost two thousand years until the Dewey Decimal Classification was created in 1876.

18 The theory is that as basic needs and requirements are met, humans can focus on self-actualizing, self-developing activities. The five "needs", in the order of basic to less basic are: Physiological (Food, Air, Water), Safety (Shelter, Clothing, Community), Love/Belonging (Healthy Relationships), Self-Esteem (acceptance of self), Self-Actualization (Feeling fulfilled).

[19] *"If those books are in agreement with the Quran, we have no need of them; and if these are opposed to the Quran, destroy them."*—A quote attributed to Omar, an influential Muslim Caliph

[20] A thoroughly brilliant and highly annotated read on the Fall of the Library of Alexandria (http://bit.ly/ttwdkf13)

[21] Elbert Hubbard, *Little Journeys to the Homes of the Great Teachers, 1908*

[22] All practicing Jews were required to pay a tax after the First Jewish-Roman war (66 CE—73 CE). The concept of a religious tolerance tax is not concentrated here. Throughout history, we've seen this tax applied at different times with different groups. Muslims invading India required non-Muslims to pay this tax as well, called *"jizya"*

[23] Attributed to Jean-Christophe BENOIST, CC BY 2.5 (http://bit.ly/2u8q42i)

[24] The Tetrarchy divided the rule of the Roman Empire among four individuals. An Augustus and a Caesar in the west and in the east each. Augusti were the co-emperors of the Empire,

with Caesars supported them as junior emperors and had a right of succession.

[25] An official position of the roman army. Used as a stepping stone to the Roman Senate.

[26] By Decius in 250 CE

[27] One source, by Lactantius, suggests that while Diocletian was already weakened, Galerius manipulated him into resigning.

[28] An interesting read on how Constantine's early life shaped his development (http://bit.ly/ttwdk22)

[29] Gaul was the general region of present day France, Luxembourg, Belgium, parts of Switzerland and Italy

[30] The Nicene Creed came out of the first council of Nicaea, a gathering of Christian bishops to resolve and reconcile the differences that arose in the Church of Alexandria. The two chief concerns were the nature of God the Son, and when to celebrate Easter.

31 Ben House, "It Takes a Monk to Save a Civilization" (http://bit.ly/ttwdwkf26)

32 How the Irish Saved Civilization, Thomas Cahill, 1995

33 There are a number of women who practiced and contributed to the fields of philosophy, physics, astronomy and botany, among others. An ever-growing list of names and histories can be found on Wikipedia (http://bit.ly/ttwdkf28)

34 Bhatt, Rakesh Kumar (1995). *History and Development of Libraries in India*. Mittal Publications. ISBN 8170995825.

35 Decimal system is the system of numbers with the base 10. Most cultures devised a numerical system with base 10, probably because we have ten fingers. There are exceptions— for instance, Mayans used base 20, perhaps adding up ten fingers and ten toes. This decimal *positional* system, may have been possible in India because of another invention of the same era. A Jain text, *Lokavibhaga,* is the earliest record of

the concept of the numeral zero. In this text, zero is notated by the word *Shunya,* meaning void or empty

36 Brahmagupta was the first mathematician to use zero and represent it as a number, and also to create negative and positive numbers. The concept of *zero* itself is considered to have been independently devised by the Babylonians, Mayans and the Indians, but never used as a numeral until Brahmagupta added a dot representing 0 under the number, to denote a multiplication by 10.

37 Another way to look at it is that though we may see "emptiness" or empty space, it may just be something that our senses cannot process. Dark matter, for example, is a type of matter about which we can theorize, but we don't know whether it exists, even though its existence may explain a number of observations, such as the speed of the expansion of our universe.

38 Elizabeth R. Mackenzie; Birgit Rakel (2006). *Complementary and Alternative Medicine for Older Adults: A Guide to Holistic Approaches to Healthy Aging.* Springer. p. 215. ISBN 9780826138064.

39 Walser, Joseph (2005). *Nāgārjuna in Context: Mahāyāna Buddhism and Early Indian Culture.* Columbia University Press. p. 102. ISBN 023113164X.

40 Peter Harvey, An Introduction to Buddhism ISBN 978-0-521-85942-4

41 The End of the Buddhist Monks, A.D. 1193 from Hutchinson's *Story of the Nations.*

42 Hinduism, as a religion is a western construct.

43 Basohli Miniature, Circa 1730. National Musem, New Delhi. (http://bit.ly/2te9nzB)

44 Jainism takes this belief a bit further and incorporates this into the daily actions and thoughts of its followers, so that anything we say or think is only a partially complete point of view, depending on our ultimate objective. What this means is a propagation of exceptional understanding, acceptance and compassion for the uniqueness and individuality that different people and cultures bring to life, if practiced. This also fits in very well with the *framing theory,* which we touch upon later in the book (Chapter: The Ways in Which We Lie, Section: Framing).

45 Rumi wrote extensively and reverentially about Shams-e-Tabriz, who is a Persian Muslim credited to be Rumi's spiritual inspiration.

46 The Hadith can be transliterated as a "report". It is a report of the words and actions of the Islamic Prophet Mohammed, among other things. While the Quran is the scripture accepted by all sects of Islam, the hadith differs from sect to sect, with a proportion of people rejecting the validity of the Hadith altogether.

47 "The Beginning of the Paper Industry", MuslimHeritage.com (http://bit.ly/ttwdkf33)

48 Goffman, E., 1974, *Frame analysis: An essay on the organization of experience*, London, Harper and Row.

49 31% of our land, forested, is just over 4 billion hectares. Data based on research compiled in 2010 by Earth Policy Institute from UN Food and Agriculture Organization. The figures above are from 1990 to 2010; the source of the figures in the facts is the same.

50 One way to share these facts differently is: The rate at which we cut our forests has decreased from 1990 to 2010. We discarded about 13 million hectares of foreign land per year in the 2010s, 16 million in 1990s. This *frame* suggests that we are cutting down fewer forests (true), therefore we are working towards reducing the threat from deforestation (may or may not be true).

51 An atom is made up of protons, neutrons and electrons. Quarks make up protons and neutrons, and along with leptons, they make up the building blocks of matter. Aristotle rejected the idea of atoms, and until 1800s, when this idea was revived again, we couldn't prove that atoms existed. A fairly basic introduction to Leptons and Quarks is at http://bit.ly/ttwdkf38

52 The 2012 survey looked at 1000 adults in the United States. The survey collated results for belief in ghosts and life after death, among other things. (http://bit.ly/ttwdkf42)

53 Sourced from the Myths Encyclopedia. The website contains a large amount of mythical literature, and makes for some interesting reading. (http://bit.ly/ttwdkf43)

54 Attributed to many inventors, and most commonly to Lippershey in 1608.

55 Some theories disagree. There are theories that assert that the world may exist only if it has an observer; that it doesn't exist independent of an observer.

Acknowledgements

Rikki Porwal, for critically reviewing my work and being my de facto editor, and asking me the tough questions that made this work possible.

Roop Betala, Ratna Betala, and Ritika Betala for literally everything they did. From critically reviewing to promoting my work, to supporting and encouraging me, especially when the going got tough.

Anuj Garg, Mallya Siddharth, Mark Bruns, and Ee Wen Tay for going through the very, very rough drafts and providing me with necessary guidance. Erico De Sousa Cardoso, Viveck Panjabi, Gaurav Shetty, Hardik Katira, Varun Jain, Nina Terol for supporting me and spreading the word about this book

Dennis Lim, for reminding me that I should promote and market my own work.

Pexels.com, Canva, Iconmonstr.com for their design products, images, and icons. The public domain, users on Wikipedia, Quora, and Reddit for the free distribution and sharing of knowledge.

And everyone else who supported and encouraged me, and made this possible, thank you very much.

A note regarding the images in this book

All images used in this book are either:

- In the Public Domain in the United States, and other countries where the copyright term is 100 years or less, or,
- Are licensed under Creative Commons as "Share Alike".

All footnotes refer to the original source of the images, as well as any copyright/creative commons notices required.

If, for any reason, you find that images included in this text violate copyright, please let the author know at tarun@tarunbetala.com

About the Author

Tarun Betala is the author of The Things We Don't Know. Since 2005, Tarun has published several poems, essays and short stories.

Over the last three decades, Tarun has lived in 4 countries across the world and his passion to explore the world has brought him to more than twenty countries.

Currently working in the Financial Data world, Tarun lives in Singapore with his wife. He writes extensively on tarunbetala.com. You can find Tarun on twitter at @trbetala.

You can connect with Tarun at:

- Email: tarun@tarunbetala.com
- Facebook: www.facebook.com/thethingswedontknowbook
- Twitter: www.twitter.com/trbetala
- Instagram: www.instagram.com/tarunbetala
- Youtube: www.youtube.com/tarunbetala
- Website: www.tarunbetala.com

98598909R00098

Made in the USA
Columbia, SC
02 July 2018